THE
CONSULTANT'S
HANDBOOK

THE
CONSULTANT'S
HANDBOOK

How to Start and Develop Your Own Practice

SECOND EDITION

Stephan Schiffman

Adams Media Corporation
Holbrook, Massachusetts

Published by
Adams Media Corporation
260 Center Street, Holbrook, MA 02343
www.adamsmedia.com

ISBN: 1-58062-441-3

Printed in Canada.

J I H G F E D C B A

Library of Congress Cataloging-in-Publication Data
available from the publisher.

This publication is designed to provide accurate and authoritative information with
regard to the subject matter covered. It is sold with the understanding that the publisher is not engaged in rendering legal, accounting, or other professional advice. If
legal advice or other expert assistance is required, the services of a competent professional person should be sought.
　　—From a *Declaration of Principles* jointly adopted by a Committee of the
American Bar Association and a Committee of Publishers and Associations.

Cover photo by Bill Losh/FPG International.

This book is available at quantity discounts for bulk purchases.
For information, call 1-800-872-5627.

Dedication

To D.M.S. and J.R.S.

Contents

| CONTENTS |

Acknowledgments

My thanks to the following: For shaping the raw material and molding it into a new, vital, and different book, my editor Brandon Toropov; for her help in both reviewing the final manuscript and providing continuous input throughout the editorial process, Kate Layzer; for asking the right questions, offering encouragement, and keeping the material firmly based in reality, my students over the years; for their unending moral and logistical help, the staff and faculty of the New School for Social Research; for her support, Anne; and for actually going out there and making it work, the professional consultants all across the country who've made this field one of the most exciting on today's business scene.

Introduction

In 1979, I started a consulting firm with about $20,000 of borrowed money, which I promptly lost. When I say promptly, I mean it. The process of going from $20,000 to zero took three months, tops. (This was in Carter Administration dollars, mind you!)

About six months into the hectic and demanding job of keeping my new business afloat, I realized that there were quite a few things about consulting that no one had told me. These were basic issues having to do with marketing, billing, cash projection, and other impossible-to-ignore challenges. I had to learn about them the hard way, by making mistakes and patching together solutions after the fact to the best of my ability. Fortunately, I learned from those errors, and the business I started eventually grew into a global sales training firm that numbers among its clients some of the most prestigious members of the Fortune 500.

The point of this book is a simple one: You don't have to learn the way I did.

Over the years, I've given seminars on consulting to a great many groups. The participants have been people from all walks of life. By taking my course, they learned about the practical problems that confront anyone attempting to start a new business as a consultant ... and they learned about the approaches I took to resolving those problems. This book is based on those seminars. It is meant to answer the questions you are now asking—or soon will ask—if you're seriously considering a career as a consultant. What should you know about establishing a practice? How do you attract and keep customers? How do you determine what fees to charge? What should a proposal look like? How much money will you need to start out?

In tackling these questions, I have drawn on my own business experience with prospects, clients, and banks, and done my level best to explain how I've addressed these challenges in my own firm. Although my area of expertise may well be very different from yours, I believe that the same fundamental challenges are common to just about every type of consulting work. So whether you're an electrical engineer or an expert on Internet startups, what follows should be of use to you as you start and nurture your consulting practice.

That having been said, I do want to say that I cannot decide for you whether or not you should become a consultant in the first place. Only you can do that. What I can do, however, is show you the strategies and internal tools you'll need to pursue a career in this demanding, rewarding business. After you read the book, I believe you'll be in a good position to decide whether or not this way of working is for you.

If you are cut out for a career as a consultant, and if you apply the ideas within this book, you'll be in a great position to reap the many benefits that this line of work has to offer. You may already be familiar with some of these benefits. In fact, they may have inspired you to buy this book in the first place! They include: independence; opportunity; a chance to express your entrepreneurial spirit; freedom from the numbing difficulties that often accompany work within one company structure; immediate exposure to the bottom-line issues that affect your business; and the chance to work, at your own pace, on the work you enjoy the most and are most adept at performing.

Read this book carefully. Study every suggestion as it relates to your new consulting business and never forget that that business will be based on your skills and unique qualifications—no one else's. You must offer energy, intelligence, perseverance, and (last but not least) specialized knowledge. In the pages that follow, I will do my best to provide relevant experience from the front lines. If that experience is of use to you in starting and nurturing your consulting business, then this book will have served its purpose.

For more help, and for ideas on what to do once you've completed this book, please visit our World Wide Web site: *www.dei-sales.com.*

—Stephan Schiffman

CHAPTER 1

What Do You Do?

The Two Big Goals and the Three Nasty Myths

Why do you want to go into consulting?

There are two main reasons that most people give—and both reasons are very good ones. The first is making money. And the second is freedom.

These are perfectly legitimate goals that can in fact be achieved during the course of a consulting career, but (isn't there always a "but" around here?) you should, before you go any further, know something important about the line of work you've chosen. Those goals of money and freedom are really only attainable if you go about attaining them from an informed point of view. That means you have to avoid potentially career-shattering myths. There are, as it turns out, three particularly dangerous myths that surround the field of consulting.

I want to explode them, because they are the most dangerous obstacles to a strong career decision on your part. These three myths are probably the most tangible causes of career unhappiness that there are in the field. If you hear someone repeat, with a straight face, any of the myths below, respond with the facts I've laid out after each one.

Here goes.

Myth Number One:

Once you embark upon a career as a consultant you need never worry about the difficulties many other people have with working for bosses. You're your own boss.

Fact: One of the big advantages to hiring a consultant is that a company is not dealing with a full-time employee. Consultants are hired for specific tasks and for specific periods, with no guarantees. As a result, their clients have no qualms whatsoever about firing them if a job is not working out as planned—or even if the company's strategy changes unexpectedly! Consultants have many, many bosses—and are, if anything, *more* sensitive about keeping them happy than are other workers.

Myth Number Two:

Consultants are highly-respected members of the professional community, like doctors and lawyers, and as such need only announce the opening of their practice to ensure steady business.

Fact: Consultants who ignore the marketing aspects of their business do not stay consultants for very long. If you can't identify your market and figure out a realistic strategy for reaching it, you are marked for failure.

Myth Number Three:

Being a consultant is, by the very nature of the job, less stress-oriented and time-sensitive than most other fields. When you're a consultant, you can write your own hours and work as little or as much as you want—and still be successful.

Fact: Consultants who look forward to a lifetime of getting up at noon and remembering the bad old days when they had to meet deadlines are in for a big disappointment.

Consultants offer solutions to business problems—and work for businesspeople. On someone else's terms and under very real time constraints, consultants tend to work hard to meet honest-to-goodness deadlines.

Disillusioned? Don't be. If you're looking for a way to channel skills and expertise on a given subject directly into a business problem—without worrying about long-term career politics, stultifying job descriptions, and constant personality problems with one or two omnipresent supervisors—consulting can be a godsend. And, with work and dedication, you can make a very good living at it. As long as you don't try to live by the myths.

Determining Your Specialty

What is it that you plan to offer your clients?

I'm making an assumption in writing this book. I'm assuming you're fantastic. I assume that if you're contemplating beginning a practice, you already possess a strong set of skills or a noted expertise in a certain area. If you don't, you can't realistically expect someone to pay you for your services.

It's possible, though, that you need a little bit more in the way of definition before you proceed with this book. I can't tell you what you do best—that's something you'll need to decide. And to help you with that, I'm providing here a quick summary of the various types of people who can realistically expect, with hard work, to make a success of themselves in the field of consulting. If you're not on the list, it doesn't mean you can't be a consultant. It does mean that you should take a good look at your skills, background, and expertise, and come up with a solid "package" that a client will view as a realistic option for a solution to tangible business problems.

Teachers or social workers well versed in solving problems or "showing others the ropes" in a certain field, comfortable working with others, and eager to provide answers to questions that arise among coworkers and pupils.

Academics hoping to put abstract research or technical training to practical application.

Retired or soon-to-be-retired executives with significant problem-solving or management skills that are easily transferred to a new business environment.

Managers, trainers, or analysts whose present positions do not afford them the opportunity for producing tangible business results or performing to the fullest—or *skilled troubleshooters* within a company who work best outside of a strict hierarchy.

Those wishing to reenter the workforce after an absence from it, but unwilling to commit their previous experience in a given field to a full-time office position.

Entrepreneurs with hands-on ability who want to work on the "firing line" of a new business, dealing directly with customers and their real-life business problems.

Technical specialists who can make new (or, in some settings, old) computer tools and applications make sense to those who lack hands-on knowledge in a certain area. Specifically, those with knowledge about Internet and World Wide Web applications of interest to organizations expanding their online presence.

What's in a Name?

I would suggest that you take a couple of moments at this point and, if you have not already done so, select a name for your consulting firm. Why? Once you've named your business, it becomes a concrete entity in your mind—something worth making plans for, something you can discuss realistically with other people.

What should you name your company? It's up to you. You can, if your name is Stephan Schiffman, call your company Schiffman Associates. Or Stephan Schiffman Consultants. Or

The Schiffman Company. These are all common enough approaches.

But you don't have to do it that way. If your main service is going to be offering design analysis services for manufacturers of widgets, you could call yourself Widget Design and Engineering. Of course, if you are extremely sensitive about some kind of proprietary element or patent question on the service you'll be offering, you may shy away from mentioning the actual service in the company name. That's fine. It's also a perfectly acceptable technique to call your company something that has absolutely nothing to do with your business: The XYZ Company. I would recommend giving a potential client some idea of what it is that you do from the moment he or she picks up your business card—but if you elect to try something else, you are in very good company.

Whatever you decide on, grab a notebook or a loose piece of paper and a pen, and write down your company's name. And, while you're at it, why not jot down a couple of brief sentences that outline what it is that you do, and what group of people you expect to be most likely to pay for it? We'll come back to what you've written a little later.

Incorporation and Other Legalities

Legally speaking, what *is* XYZ Company—or whatever it is you're calling your practice?

Let's start with some basics. I'm a businessman. Because I'm a businessman, I can give you a solid perspective on the pros and cons of incorporation. I can also offer you some follow-up advice on the matter: Make the wise investment of time and money required to speak with an attorney about starting up your business. He or she will be able to take into account all the particulars of your situation, inform you of the specific requirements of your state and local government, and tell you honestly what your wisest course is. It may cost you at the beginning, but remember: You're starting a business. Take the time. Do it right.

So, let's examine the options. Broadly speaking, there are three: You can operate as a *sole proprietorship;* you can form a *partnership;* or you can opt for *incorporation.*

From my point of view, and speaking strictly from my own experience, I've found that operating under a sole proprietorship or as a partnership makes more sense than incorporating a consulting business. Why? Because the primary motive behind forming a corporation—which is a kind of artificial person from a legal standpoint—is to construct an entity that absorbs liability in the event of a lawsuit.

In other words, if you manufacture motorcycle helmets you may be concerned about becoming the target of lawsuits initiated by people who may be injured while using your product. But the entity being sued will depend on the entity that produced the motorcycle helmet in the first place.

If you, John Smith, sole proprietor, produced the motorcycle helmets, then the person claiming that your helmets were unsafe will sue you.

If you, John Smith, and your partner, Mary Brown, produced the motorcycle helmets together as part of a partnership, then you and Ms. Brown will be the targets of the lawsuit.

And if JS Helmets, Incorporated produced the motorcycle helmets, then JS Helmets Incorporated will be sued. You, John Smith—your bank account, the equity you've built up in your home, your assets—are completely distinct from the company (with the exception, of course, of your status as an officeholder). In our hypothetical lawsuit, the *company's* money is at stake, and not your own—because, strictly speaking, you did not make the motorcycle helmets. JS Helmets, Incorporated did.

So if the corporation is so much of a shield in such situations, why do I prefer to operate as a sole proprietor? Because

I'm a consultant. I don't make motorcycle helmets. I don't *make* anything. I offer a service. And because I offer a service, the risks traditionally associated with manufacturing businesses are not as common. Many consulting practices, accordingly, operate as sole proprietorships rather than corporations.

Partnerships, too, may be an attractive option for you. If there are two people operating the business—if, for instance, John Smith intends to handle most of the marketing, while Mary Brown will actually provide the services to the clients—then a partnership might make the most sense. In either instance, you can name your company XYZ Associates without incorporating—simply by contacting the appropriate office of your state government and filling out the forms that will allow you to operate under that company name. Your full company name might be something like "John Smith and Mary Brown, partners, doing business as XYZ Associates."

A Hint That May Help You Save on Taxes

There is another option you may wish to consider: It's called a "Sub-Chapter S" corporation. If you're worried about liability, such a corporation offers you the expected protection of your personal assets, but also allows you the advantage of being taxed as an individual—at least where the federal government is concerned.

Some states tax this type of corporation exactly as they would any other. In any event, if you select this course, you will need to provide an income statement and a complete balance sheet for both state and federal purposes. (A sole proprietorship or a partnership is only required to submit an income statement.)

Now that we've taken a very broad look at this question, let me reiterate my advice. Go see an attorney. (You may find laws in this area changing unexpectedly.) Then make your decision, carry out the paperwork properly, and you'll be—quite literally—in business.

The Worst-Case Scenario

What's the worst thing that could happen to you and your plans to begin a consulting business?

I don't ask that question flippantly—I honestly want you to consider what may be in store if your plans don't work out at first. I've already mentioned in the Introduction how I lost $20,000 in a little less than sixty working days. Think about that. Think about your plans. And ask yourself—what is the worst thing that could happen?

You could fail.

It's not a big deal. Say it out loud. You could fail. Then what? Then you'd start over again. Try something new. Bring the experience you've earned to a new business, maybe try a different field.

It happens every day. R. H. Macy had to start seven different stores before he hit on his winning formula. The business sections of newspapers have always been full of such stories. There are reference books in most public libraries—huge, musty volumes, just crammed with the names of all the bankrupt and defunct businesses that have called it quits over the years.

You are embarking on the job of starting a new business. Start that job by taking an honest look at the numbers. Look at all of the people behind all of the businesses listed in those books who failed—and found something else. They can't all have jumped out of eighteenth-story windows, right?

Why do I bring this up? Because I want to give you the proper perspective on the business end of consulting. The fact of the matter is that something in the neighborhood of 95 percent of all new businesses are *out* of business within one year of opening their doors.

So why consulting? Well, the beauty of this business is that, if you have to, you can start it with one employee—you. You will work. Very hard. But you can get a consulting operation up and running and find that you've made a very respectable start without involving a lot of other people in the project. What that means is that if you fail, you haven't displaced dozens of workers, left a hole in the neighborhood you worked in, or deserted benefits and pension plans people are counting on. All you've done is added a line to your resume! And if your financial planning is realistic (and I've devoted a later chapter to help you make sure it is), you won't have to go looking for a window to jump out of.

The "Screaming Baby"

We come now to the toughest part of beginning a consulting practice.

Of course, we've already talked a little about how you're the only one who can determine precisely *what* it is that you do. Now, how do we boil that information down into a convincing, concise summation of your business? What can you say that will immediately convey to the potential client all that you have to offer?

Take a moment to go back to your notes. Review the name you've given your company and the description of what you do.

Ask yourself this question: If I were a potential client with a dozen uncompleted tasks begging for my attention, and someone sat down next to me one afternoon and read me, word-for-word, what is on this piece of paper, would I drop what I was doing and ask to hear more about the service?

Be honest. Note that you're not asking whether or not you'd *pay* for the service. Only whether you'd stop your activities and pay attention for a moment.

Dr. Benjamin Spock, instructing a young editor who was to oversee a new edition of his book *Baby and Child Care,* once addressed the same issue. Dr. Spock told the editor, "Picture a mother with a screaming baby in one hand and the book in the other."

Does your description get straight to the point? Does it tell the potential client—*immediately*—how your service will benefit him or her? If it doesn't, you're in trouble.

Picture an executive with a "screaming baby"—a business problem *that you can solve*—bellowing into his or her ear. How much time, realistically, do you have to get to the heart of the matter and communicate the fact that you have a solution to that problem? A minute? Thirty seconds? Fifteen seconds?

Most beginning consultants fail to show the proper respect for a potential client's time in their service descriptions. They'll ask people to do business with them on the basis of something like this:

> **The MCS Group.** Founded in 1987 by Michael Collins Stemway (who plans to continue to serve as president for the foreseeable future), the MCS Group represents a fresh approach to a field long plagued by indecision, vague expression, and obtuseness. Why? The answer is simple. The MCS Group is different. Really different. Where other firms will waffle on the important issues, MCS delivers. How? By bringing fresh perspectives. New ideas. Unique approaches. And the kind of attention to detail that's made us one-of-a-kind. Think we're exaggerating? Try this on for size: MCS Group supplies all its clients with written copies of all our performance assessments from past assignments, so that the proper personnel can make informed decisions about motivational seminars. That's MCS Group. That's different.

Now. If you're sitting there with the "screaming baby" (in this case, say, a listless and unmotivated sales staff) howling away, and someone asks you to listen for a moment on the basis of the description above, what's your reaction? *It's a waste of your time!* Even if you do take the trouble to read all the way to the end and deduce that the firm seems to have something to do with seminars designed to motivate your staff—how on earth can you convince yourself that this firm has any respect for your problems? They spend the whole paragraph chattering about themselves! What do they have to offer you? On the basis of the description above (which, believe it or not, isn't too far from some descriptions I've seen), the answer is a simple one. Nothing.

One Big Idea

Identify an area of potential savings or enhancement of profits for your client. And then, in two short sentences, illustrate how your service will either save your client money or enhance his company's sales—or both.

Two sentences. That's how much time you have. But, if you think about it, it's plenty of time. It's an eternity. If you have your potential client's attention.

Think along the lines of descriptions like these:

> MCS Group specializes in analyzing unproductive work groups, developing and administering motivational activities, and increasing employee productivity. We turn clock-watchers into profit-minded team players.

> Smith Associates generates legally mandated reports for pharmaceutical firms on new products. Our experts can cost-effectively produce reports for submission to the Food and Drug Administration

without taxing a company's development, editorial, research, or art departments.

XYZ Associates is a sales training firm. Our methods can teach your sales staff to spend less time with dead-end prospects and close more sales per hour.

Now take a moment to look closely at your own description of what you'll do for the client. Try to rework it along the lines of the ones I've given you above. When you've completed that, take another sheet of paper and write down three "hows"—the specific things you'll be doing and tactics you'll be using to *carry out* the objectives outlined in your two-sentence description.

The descriptions I've given you will probably have the most influence a little later on, when you begin putting together your marketing plan. But for now, use the three examples above to streamline how you think about what you want your consulting business to do. Tailor your vision of your firm to one person's perspective: the client's. Believe me, it will pay off.

Defining Yourself

Here is where we come to one of the big secrets of a successful consulting practice. It's a very simple idea, and the only reason it remains a secret is that so many beginning (and not-so-beginning) consultants refuse to employ it.

You are what you sell the client. And you are selling a benefit.

You're not selling your smile, handshake, or grey flannel suit. You're not selling your stationery. You're not selling your office decor.

Even if there's nothing you can physically put your hand on and say, "I made this," you're selling a *product*. Fair enough. What's the product? Well, think about it. You're solving a problem. The solution to that problem *is* your product.

By this point you probably have a pretty good idea of what problems you will be attempting to solve. Now all you have to do is remember: *You're selling that solution because it is of recognizable benefit to a business.*

Some people sell cars. Some people sell computers. Some people sell lemonade from a stand on the sidewalk. In your case, you are selling *the answer to someone's prayers.* Not a report. Not a series of interviews. Not a graph.

When you recognize the fact that you're identifying a problem, using your expertise and ability, and delivering a *solution,* you're well on your way to becoming a successful consultant.

Consider other products that people buy—and why they buy them. Consider, say, green rubber boots. Why do people buy green rubber boots? Well now. *What* are they actually buying? You could come up with a list of things *connected* with green rubber boots: the color, the lining, the strength of the seams, the thickness of the soles. But are these the actual *product,* in a fundamental sense? I say no. I say they're *features.* They're part of the *why.* They aren't the *what.*

There's another important element that enters into any discussion about the green rubber boots: the manufacturer's reputation. The fact that the product has good "word-of-mouth," or that the company that makes the green rubber boots has been in business for forty years, regularly getting top marks in *Consumer Reports.*

But, again, that's only a contributing factor to the decision to buy green rubber boots. It's a very important part: the *proof.* But it's not what someone actually purchases. It's still part of the *why.*

Think of the *problem* solved by a pair of green rubber boots. You're stranded at rush hour in front of a shoe store. It's pouring out. You're wearing a pair of sneakers. Your feet are five minutes away from being completely soaked. You look in the window and see a beautiful pair of green rubber boots. You decide you can afford them. You walk in and buy a pair. *What have you really bought?*

Dry feet!

That's the *benefit* of green rubber boots. That's what the shoe store really has for sale.

What is the *result* that your consulting business provides? What saves a client money? Makes his or her business more productive? Creates more profit? Whatever it is, that's your *product*. That's the *benefit*. The *benefit* is different from *how* the savings, productivity, or profit is delivered. *How* is interesting—and important—but it's not the product.

Let's review this idea. It's an important one, and you'll become intimately acquainted with it as you enter into the realm of marketing your services. From the customer's (read: client's) point of view, the whole question of "to buy or not to buy" boils down to a simple three-way analysis—a triangle, if you will, with the *benefit* at the apex.

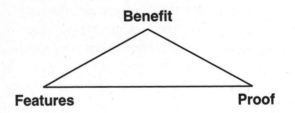

Benefit

Features   **Proof**

Benefit (you get home with dry feet). *Features* (thick soles). *Proof* (your sister-in-law swears by these rubber boots).

Try it with your consulting service.

Benefit (motivated and more productive sales staff). *Features* (analysis of staff and customized seminars). *Proof* (your years of experience and your previous satisfied customers).

We'll deal with both features and proof in much more detail later on. For now, I want you to understand the importance of the benefit you offer a client. It's completely synonymous with your product. It defines you as a consultant.

So—have you identified the benefit you offer to prospective clients? Review your written summary of what you do right now. If that summary does not contain a clear benefit statement, you should complete another draft of it before you read any further.

The Classic Pattern; or, What You Have to Look Forward to over the Next Three Years

Now that you've identified for yourself and your potential client exactly what it is that you do, you should probably take note of the patterns that emerging consulting businesses typically undergo in their first few years. The best reason for taking some time now to examine these patterns is to allow you to anticipate problems associated with growth—ahead of time. You may not be able to counteract these tendencies completely, but if you're well prepared, you'll be a step ahead of the game.

Let's assume you're a fantastic consultant. (If you're assuming anything less, you're wasting your time!) Let's assume that you're beginning your practice from scratch—and that you're so phenomenal at what you do, you apply so completely the principles that you'll learn in this book, that your business makes it well past that magic one-year mark by which nineteen out of twenty fail. What do the first, say, three years look like for you?

They look something like this.

Year One: Crisis

The game is survival, plain and simple. Basic, nagging questions have a nasty habit of popping up again and again.

Was your plan correct? Did you secure enough financing? Why didn't you anticipate this or that cost? How are you going to pay the rent? Why don't people pay you on time? Was leaving your old job really worth this? How long is it going to take you to make some real money?

Now, if you're attentive, you'll notice something very interesting about all those questions—and the dozens more just like them that will, more than likely, wake you up in the middle of the night during the course of the first year. You'll notice that they have virtually nothing to do with providing top-notch, professional service to your clients—which is what you *must* do in your first year to build a client base and a reputation.

So we've come upon the fundamental conflict of the first year. You must nurture and maintain your business through some extremely difficult moments, without ever losing sight of why you're consulting: to help your clients. If you attend to the former and lose sight of the latter, you will not build a client base. On the other hand, of course, if you neglect such "details" as paying the rent on your office space, you will not have a business.

So how do you pull it off? Easy. Just step into a phone booth and change into your Superman costume.

Seriously, though, you may want to ask yourself if you're up to handling the pressures of seeing a business through its first year—on your own. If you're not, that does *not* mean that you can't be a consultant. All it means is that you may want to consider a partnership, or the option of hiring substantial accounting, clerical, or billing help from the beginning. That, of course, costs money, and detracts from the "on my own" mystique of the business you've chosen for yourself. But the help may well be worth it.

You could conclude that you *are* cut out for handling these problems solo. Lots of consultants have done so with great success. But know what you're taking on *before* you decide to take it on.

Year Two: Ecstasy and Expansion

You've done it! You've made it past the first year—and you're part of that five-percent elite.

Somehow, you've proven your ability to manage the conflicts inherent in holding a number of important roles simultaneously—operations manager, salesperson, expert in your field, solver of client problems, and chief executive officer. Now that you've seen your business take root and, dare I say it, grow, what are you going to do? Sit there and rest on your laurels? Or try to find a way to get things moving even faster?

You wouldn't have gone into consulting in the first place if you wanted to stagnate. You could have done that at any old job. So in the second year, perhaps even without consciously setting out to do so, the tendency is to spread out. Find new areas to serve your clients. Maybe hire a few new people. Make a real name for your firm.

Which, more than likely, you do. With some success until . . .

Year Three: Overextension

Suddenly, things seem to fall apart no matter how many problems you solve. Those few extra people you hired complicate matters more than you thought they would. The simple step of hiring a receptionist means—gulp—someone else is talking to the clients before you are! Sure, you could do without the constant hassle of answering the phone, but what do you do when you find out that someone who represents a good sixth of your yearly revenue is left on hold for twenty minutes?

All of a sudden, what with all the expansion and hiring, you've got overhead costs you wouldn't have dreamed of a year or two back. Was that what you had in mind when you started your career as a consultant?

And that business of finding a new specialty or two. It sure looked good on paper, but now you find that the time you've taken to get things rolling didn't just come out of nowhere. It meant that you had less time to follow up on contacts from your previous jobs—something that was second nature during the first year.

Your company checkbook is a mess. You used to balance it like clockwork, once a month. Now it seems no matter what you do, you're working from eight in the morning until seven or so at night—and you're *still* not caught up with the basics!

It's called growth. And it happens to every business that succeeds. How's that for a paradox? The more you grow, the more chaos you seem to create! Some reward!

Obviously, you're not *fated* to follow these patterns. But you should realize that it's a common experience for thousands of consultants. Read this book, make a solid plan based on the problems you can realistically expect to encounter—and then play to win.

CHAPTER 2

Who Needs What You Have to Offer?

The Magic Phone

Several years ago, a good friend of mine began a career as a consultant. He had a very impressive resume, with credentials that included an advanced degree from one of the top universities in the country. One day, I dropped by his office to see how the new venture was going.

As I walked in, I heard total silence. No work was being done. I stepped into my friend's room, only to find him staring philosophically at the telephone.

We exchanged hellos and, after a little chitchat, I asked him what he was up to, and why he was spending his time in front of the phone. Was he expecting an important call from a particular client?

"Oh, no," came the answer. "No one in particular. I just know people are going to start calling now and I don't want to miss them when they phone."

I looked at my friend. Then I looked at the wall where he'd hung his advanced degree from one of the top universities in the country. Then I looked back at my friend. I came away with the conclusion that one of two things had taken place during the course of my friend's education. Either he had learned how to construct a magic telephone that would automatically deliver qualified prospects to his waiting ear—or he had not learned much about marketing and its importance to a healthy consulting business. If he had acquired rights to the design for the magic phone, I'm here to tell you it was out of order on the day that I stopped by.

It's sad but true. There are a staggering number of people who think that, by virtue of a good idea or two, they can expect people to beat a path to their door. Don't expect that. If you've got a good idea and you don't tell anybody about it, *nothing's going to happen.*

We address now the question of marketing—a vitally important area for any beginning business, and certainly one that you, as a beginning consultant, must know intimately. This chapter will focus on identifying *who* your market base is; subsequent chapters will give you some ideas on *how* to conduct your marketing.

Know Your Market Base

"What's your market?"

This is a very important question. It's tempting to answer it with something that doesn't fully take into account the perspective of the client. Something like, "Anybody who's interested in improving communications among their managers." "Any business that wants to increase its sales." "Any firm that needs an analysis of its property."

Anybody: one of the most dangerous words in the English language. Why? "Anybody" doesn't exist. "Somebody" exists. A specific person, in a specific set of circumstances, with a specific problem exists. That person is who you want to reach.

Skeptical? Well, suppose you disagree. Suppose you're convinced that your personnel motivation firm really is going to appeal to "any" business, "anywhere." (It won't. But I'll make some allowances to get up a good argument.) Are you honestly willing to take on "anybody"?

The Self-Excluding Market

Let's have a look at the consequences of serving a market that consists of "anybody."

You have an office in midtown Manhattan. One morning your telephone rings—it's a businessman whose headquarters are located in West Palm Beach, Florida. He's heard wonderful things about your services from an acquaintance of his in New York. Can you come down, analyze his staff, and give one of your motivational seminars at his office in Florida?

Before you try to answer the question this little scenario poses, incorporate a couple of "givens." Assume that the conversation takes place during your first year of existence— before you've issued public stock, launched an expensive nationwide advertising campaign, and authorized franchises from coast to coast. And assume that the money you're being offered to perform this service is your standard fee. (What constitutes your standard fee? We'll cover that in a later chapter.) And, finally, assume that in order to fulfill this assignment, you will not have to cancel any of your existing business commitments in New York—as long as you're willing to catch two "redeye" flights in 72 hours, miss your daughter's third birthday party, and eat enough airline and motel food to make your stomach consider seceding from your body.

Do you take the assignment?

(If you answered "yes" to the above question, go find a three-year-old, look deep into the moppet's eyes, and say twenty times the following phrase: "Daddy doesn't love you anymore." Then, if you're not completely crushed, go back to the question and try again.)

Maybe I'm balancing the scales against you. But, by the same token, taking any and every assignment you may ever hear of does exactly that, as well—tips the scales out of your favor. By now you see my point. If you're going to be a human being at the same time that you're a consultant, you'll need some perspective in targeting your market.

To some degree, you are making marketing decisions without even meaning to! "No. I will not tear my life into little bits every two weeks. I want to work in the greater New York City area." You probably didn't *mean* to write off all the potential companies who need motivational seminars and happen to be located in Fairbanks, Alaska. But you did. All I'm saying is— make *conscious* choices. Decide *who* you will target. Know *why* you're targeting them.

I can hear you now. "That's only geography. Of course I'm not going to travel halfway across the country to fulfill one assignment. But in my own region, my market is anyone who's interested in the service!"

Is it?

Effective Use of Your Time

As a consultant, your time is, by definition, a valuable commodity. (And if you're a beginning consultant, your time is a *precious* commodity.)

That may sound like I'm stating the obvious, but sometimes the obvious ideas are the ones with the most complicated implications. Let's examine the idea of a sales cycle—the time that you set aside in your practice to prospect for new clients.

Now, the dynamic is somewhat different for a two-person consulting firm, but the fact remains: You can't prospect while you're servicing clients, and you can't service clients while you're prospecting. Typically, you'll do one at the expense of the other, wake up in a cold sweat one night, and switch activities after you realize what you've been neglecting. The resulting roller-coaster ride looks something like this:

Those peaks are where you realize you have no prospects (a frightening thought when you realize that you *are* hoping that you'll still be in business three months down the line). The valleys are where you realize that you have no money. Each realization, as I say, is a powerful motivator.

So the object, obviously, is to make the time that you spend prospecting as productive as humanly possible. Every wasted moment in your prospecting is a moment that could have been spent with a client—a moment you could have been paid for. You can't let those moments slip away in unproductive marketing plans.

Now, we know that there's no such thing as a magic phone. Referrals from former clients, such as the one in the scenario above, are not magic; it takes time and lots of work to build up a productive contact network. Given the fact that you are going to have to spend *some* of your time on marketing efforts, how can you ensure that the time you're spending is the most *productive* time?

Let me steer you toward an answer to that question by posing another one. If your consulting service offers personnel analysis and motivational training, does it make sense for you to target companies with ten employees or fewer?

No. Why not? Well, companies with ten employees or fewer tend to have pretty open lines of communication. If the boss is unhappy with someone's performance, he or she is in a fairly good position to call the person into his or her office—or call a quick meeting with the relevant department. It would be tough to sell personnel analysis services to the president of a small company. Not impossible, but tough. The service you'd be asking the company to pay for probably wouldn't address a real, everyday problem.

What about companies of five hundred employees or more, then?

Now we've hit on something. Productivity, morale, and profit-orientation are major, ongoing issues addressed regularly by large companies. With all the different departments and seemingly endless layers of bureaucracy in a big organization, it's often impossible to keep track of everyone. People get cut off from their customers. People perform tasks and lose sight of the purpose of their efforts. People lose their initiative, keep an eye on the clock, and sometimes even spend their time trying to find ways *not* to do the work that's on their schedule.

Could you offer personnel analysis and motivation services to a large company with those kinds of problems—and realistically offer to improve their productivity and profitability?

Yes, you could. And if that's the kind of consulting you offer, that's exactly the kind of company you should try to locate.

You *could* try to find "any" company that needed such services. But in the process, you'd spend a lot of time with smaller firms that, at least 90 percent of the time, would reject you. And you would *waste your time.* So why not isolate the kind of company that typically needs your services—and spend your time with those firms?

Take a good long look at what you offer. Ask yourself whom your service appeals to. And ask yourself honestly what setting your service operates most effectively in. Then make some choices.

My company, for instance, offers sales training services. However, the services we offer are geared to larger sales staffs that make a comparatively modest number of high-dollar sales per rep. In other words, my seminars aren't really geared to help out a company with three telemarketers trying to sell newspaper subscriptions. That's not my market. So whom do we target? Companies that are within a hundred miles of New York City, generate a minimum of $100 million in annual sales, and employ at least ten sales representatives. That's my market.

What's yours?

The Shrinking Pool

The table below might represent a typical progression for many beginning consulting firms going through the steps necessary to target a market. Note how the "pool" of potential clients is isolated with greater and greater precision as the market is defined.

Anybody

Companies That Need Personnel Evaluation
and Motivation Seminars

Companies with Large Workforces

Companies Employing 500 or More

Companies Employing 500 or More Within a
Two-Hour Drive of New York City

Companies or Divisions Engaged in a Service Industry,
Generating Gross Revenue of at Least $50 million, with
White-Collar Employment of at Least 300,
Within a Two-Hour Drive of New York City

Note how quickly the second step is transformed. Why is there no mention of the company's "needing" your services after that second step? "Needing" is irrelevant! There is no need until you uncover a need. For all you know, the company doesn't realize that it needs a consultant yet! That's part of your marketing job—uncovering that need, identifying it. If they *knew* that they needed the services, they'd have gone out and hired someone already!

Why People Will Hire You

Now that I've convinced you—I hope—of the necessity of targeting your market, you're probably asking yourself what criteria you're going to have to set up to distinguish someone who's in your market from someone who isn't. And, to be frank, that's one of the questions you're going to have to work out on your own. Certainly, you know your field far better than I ever will.

What I can do, however, is give you some examples, and provide some insight into the mindset that accompanies a decision to hire a consultant.

Three motives tend to underlie that choice.

Motive One:

The company wants a short-term problem solved quickly, and cannot solve it with its current staff because of skill or time constraints.

Let's say a medium-size manufacturing firm has outgrown its invoicing system. The people in operations are unsure as to what a new system should be expected to accomplish: sales analysis? commission payments? monthly statements? The president is unwilling to take managers off current projects, as deadlines are looming; at any rate, none of them have in-depth experience in this area. At this point, a consultant might be hired to analyze the current workflow and recommend an existing or customized computer system that could achieve as many of the objectives of the operations department as possible.

Benefit to the company: time-sensitive analysis of the problem and recommendations based on expertise in the field—without putting other projects on hold.

Motive Two:

The company wants an objective viewpoint in order to solve an important business problem.

Assume that the A-1 Car Manufacturing Corporation has historically led the compact car market with its Zippola model. In the last couple of years, however, the Zippola's sales have dwindled. Why? That's a matter of some dispute. The sales department claims that product quality has declined, but are hard pressed to supply specifics; the engineering people insist that the salespeople just aren't doing the job. Never mind solving the problem: What *is* the problem, anyway? In a situation like this, it might make a lot of sense to hire a consultant with some background in the field, ask him or her to analyze the product and its market, and see what comes back. This kind of work takes tact and no small knowledge of what is politically possible within an organization; after all, a recommendation should be not only factually valid, but also workable!

Benefit to the company: external analysis of the problem—and expert recommendations on solving it—from someone with no position to defend in an organization's hierarchy.

Motive Three:

A company has seasonal or erratically encountered problems that are most sensibly addressed by hiring a consultant on an as-needed basis—as opposed to hiring a new full-time employee.

Repeat business is a way of life for many consultants because companies often decide that it makes more sense to fill long-term projects with one reliable consultant. Let's imagine we're part of the senior management at ABC Communications— a major player in a rapidly changing high-technology field. We're planning to open three new offices a year for the next four years, and we need to train people in every new office we open. Now, the equipment we're training people on in 2001 is not going to be the same as the equipment they'll use in 2004. But suppose we don't want to hire someone whose job it will be to analyze the equipment and training objectives; maybe we figure there are only twenty weeks of work per year at the very most in this segment of our expansion plan. Suppose we hire a consultant to help us out every time we open a new office. Wouldn't that look a lot better in the budget? (Remember: The full-timer, even though he or she may earn less per hour than the consultant, will get benefits, sick days, and vacation time—the consultant won't.)

Benefit to the company: reliable service over a period of time without committing to a full-time position.

You should also bear in mind that the size of the organization you target is of primary importance. You can keep an eye out for certain tips that will help you judge the firm's size if you lack solid information. For instance, a company that has many specialized titles (Management Information Director, Director of Customer Service, Quality Control Analyst) is almost certainly larger than one that does not. That's one way you can determine the size of an organization within seconds over the telephone!

Finding the Receptive Segment

This work is hard. Don't let anybody tell you it isn't. It's extremely difficult to break down the precise business segment

you'll be appealing to. It may be that you haven't yet suffi-
ciently isolated what service it is that you want to provide. If
that's the case, you'll probably want to go back and reex-
amine your skills and talents closely.

In any targeting decision, there are choices to be made.
The first choice you make is not to appeal to everyone on
earth. The second is to isolate that *segment* of the business
world that may be receptive to the service you're offering.
One good way to do that is to review the three main motives
for hiring a consultant that I've just outlined. Which motive
would most nearly approximate a reason that a business
would hire you? What is a distinguishing characteristic of that
type of business?

Remember the sales cycle rollercoaster. Try to make the
ride you'll eventually encounter as smooth as possible.

CHAPTER 3

How Do You Reach the Clients?

Proof

A little earlier, we discussed the concepts of benefit, features, and proof. Right now I'd like to examine the question of proof in some detail—and how you, as a beginning consultant, should provide it.

As is probably obvious to you by now, people do not buy things—or at any rate, cannot be depended upon to buy things—unless they believe they will benefit from them. Communicating that benefit is of primary importance to you. As a result, you should know that one of the first things a prospective client will look for is *proof*.

Who else have you done this for? How did it work out? How long have you been in business? Who can you give as a reference?

These are perfectly legitimate questions. They're also extremely frustrating if you're beginning a consulting practice and do not yet have a client list a yard and a half long. But before you let your frustration get the better of you, put yourself in the customer's shoes.

Suppose you were going into surgery for something—say an appendectomy. And suppose you learned, the night before the operation was scheduled to take place, that your surgeon was a young physician performing his first real operation. On you.

You probably wouldn't be in much of a mood to hear about how good the surgeon's grades were, how hard he'd studied, or how sure he was everything would turn out for the best. You'd want another doctor. And if you confronted the young surgeon, told him your feelings, and heard him explain that he "had to start with *someone*," what would your reaction be?

Not me!

Granted. It's not surgery we're discussing. But a prospective client isn't going to be much more eager to go with an untested quantity than you would be to go under the knife of that surgeon.

Catch-22

You can't get clients without a reputation. And you can't get a reputation without clients.

Or can you?

I don't want you to underestimate the difficulty of beginning a consulting practice without any client experience at all in a certain field. That's a tall order. But when you think about it, you probably have done *some* work—perhaps at a previous nine-to-five job—in your area of specialty.

If at all possible, obtain written evaluations of your work from previous contacts in the business world. Eventually, you can bind these letters—and other promotional material that presents your work in a positive light—and present the material to prospective clients. Such an "enhanced resume" will help you smooth the transition from salaried employee or professional to independent consultant, and will probably make it considerably easier to convince clients of the benefits of your service.

You can also consider building up your reputation by doing complimentary or less-than-full-fee work for local service groups or community organizations. Be sure to obtain written recommendations from these sources, as well.

To Advertise or Not to Advertise?

Zen masters, art instructors, and "method" actors are unanimous in their praise of the "first impulse." When in a difficult or challenging situation, they say, you should not "edit" your response or meditate at length about what action to pursue— you should just do it. Follow your instincts, do what comes naturally, and everything will work out all right.

This technique may be all right for acting in a scene, painting a canvas, or attaining enlightenment, but unfortunately it makes pretty lousy advice when it comes to marketing yourself as a consultant. Some first instincts definitely deserve all the scrutiny you can give them.

If I were to ask you to come up with the best way for you to market your services—and if I only gave you thirty seconds to answer—what would you say?

Advertise!

Am I right?

If so, please don't follow that impulse . . . right away. Instead, let me take a few moments to explain why advertising probably isn't the perfect vehicle for marketing a fledgling consulting practice—and outline some of the other avenues available to you.

Advertising's Drawbacks

I'm not knocking advertising as a medium. And I'm certainly not saying that it has no place in developing a consulting business. What I am saying is that for a beginning practice it's often the first method considered—maybe the only method considered. And that's a mistake, because advertising carries with it certain problems that you should be aware of.

The fact of the matter is, building your client base is the name of the game in the first year of your consulting practice, and advertising is, on the whole, a poor way to do it. There are several reasons for this. One is that advertising is often far from cost-effective. I had a friend who took out a little ad in the *New York Times* for five years straight without seeing *any* tangible results.

When I asked him why he bothered, he said he was "just keeping his name out there." That's a questionable objective even if you have an established practice, but it can be a death wish if it constitutes your strategy for generating clients in your first year. Forget "the public." You want to keep your name in front of people who might conceivably choose to pay you for what you do best.

The biggest problem with advertising someplace like the *New York Times* (as opposed to a more specialized publication, like a trade magazine) is that the typical reader is going to be totally unreceptive to paying for your services. What's the ratio going to be, realistically? One in a hundred? One in a thousand? One in ten thousand?

Remember, much of advertising's appeal in the business world lies in the results it can deliver—over a period of time and with repeated application. In other words, a campaign. Now, a campaign may deliver results for a soap company over a year or two—or three, or five. But you don't have three years. You need results *now*. (This is a point you'll probably appreciate more keenly once we discuss the issue of cash flow projections.)

Part of the cost of advertising is the amount of time it takes you to get a response that develops into a job. That cost can be prohibitively high.

If you must advertise—and you've probably guessed by now I'm advising that you look very carefully at your objectives before you do—do your best to advertise cost-effectively. In other words, isolate the trade magazines, newsletters, or talk shows that you know are popular with the specific segment of the market you want to reach, then monitor your results before continuing with the medium you've selected. Whatever you do, don't decide that everyone you want to reach watches reruns of the *Dick Van Dyke Show*, buy six months' worth of television spots, leave yourself penniless, and wait for the results to roll in. You may be doing a lot of waiting.

Think of it this way. When do *you* look at an ad? I mean really read it in depth, take note of all the prices and the descriptions. When do you take the trouble to, say, read all the fine print in a car advertisement? When you're in the market for a car—when the ad represents something of interest to you. If you're not in the market for a car (or a mattress, or a video recorder), what's your reaction to the ad? *Turn the page!*

So, is advertising a dirty word? Not necessarily. All I'm really saying is, advertising *becomes* a dirty word when it's both cost-ineffective and aimed, unwittingly, at a bunch of page-turners. Be careful. Examine all the options available to you. Above all, do not make a decision to advertise without having a rough idea of both the cost per qualified prospect that the advertising will generate and of the overall return you can expect. It's a common—and potentially deadly—mistake to overestimate the first figure and underestimate the second.

But don't despair. There are quite a few alternatives to advertising that you can opt for in designing your marketing plan. Let's take a look at them.

Word of Mouth: One on One

A gentleman by the name of Joe Girard holds the distinction of having sold three times more Chevrolets than any other human being on the planet. He made one very important discovery that enabled him to make the transition from a run-of-the-mill salesperson to a spectacular one; that discovery was deceptively simple. What did he learn?

Joe Girard learned that everybody eventually either needed a car or knew someone who did.

That's a discovery with stunning implications. In the hands of the right person, that information takes on immense economic importance. Why? Because it means that every sale Joe made was more than just a sale. It was a doorway to another sale—or sales—and a doorway to yet another doorway, to boot!

The potential of this technique in developing your customer base should be obvious. Let's say you agree to a contract with Mr. X that extends for the next three months. In reality, that's three months of interaction not only with Mr. X, but also with any people he may recommend. That may lead in turn to contracts with Ms. Y and Mr. Z. Of course, if Mr. X should *forget* to recommend these folks to you, there's no law against tactfully presenting your business card or asking if there's anyone in his field who might have use for your services.

So do that. And when Mr. X is flattered (as he probably will be) to be appealed to as an expert in his business area, be prepared to jot down any names and numbers he supplies. Always ask for permission to use Mr. X's name in contacting Ms. Y and Mr. Z—it will be a rare day when you're refused, and the effort reinforces your image as a professional.

Finally, once you do contact Ms. Y and Mr. Z, bear in mind that your call will be less of a sales pitch than a professional referral. What's the difference? A sales call is often "hard-sell" in nature and geared toward determining whether or not there is an application for your service. A referral, on the other hand, does not necessarily result in an immediate hire (although that's certainly a possibility), but rather takes advantage of the information Mr. X has supplied you with: that Ms. Y and Mr.

Z *do* have a potential application for your service. So don't pressure them. Simply inform them that their associate Mr. X suggested you give them a call, and that you've been working with him with some success on a program that's been of some real benefit to him. You think it could be equally beneficial to them, and you would like to get together in person to talk about your work with Mr. X.

Keep the call cordial, professional, and low-key. Follow the call with a very brief letter (the briefness illustrates that you understand how valuable time is) either confronting the appointment or expressing the same points you outlined in your call. Mention that you look forward to speaking with Ms. Y again sometime in the near future. Then check in by telephone every few weeks and see what happens.

As I say, there's certainly nothing to keep Mr. X from calling Ms. Y and Mr. Z on his own and recommending your service on the basis of the spectacular job you've completed. Nevertheless, you should be prepared to do some of the phone work on your own. However you slice it, you've entered upon the area most people refer to as "networking." I don't like the term because to my mind it implies exploitation on someone's part. You're not really "networking" Mr. X as much as you are:

- outlining and delivering your superior service,
- acknowledging his competence in his field by asking him to direct you to others who would be interested in your service,
- developing an ongoing business relationship with him.

Let's assume, for argument's sake, that each contact could yield three referrals, and that of those three you could convert one into a sale. How many sales could you make in six months?

That's a question that depends on your personal sales cycle, and we'll get into that a little later. But for now, let's say for the sake of argument that you make one sale in the first month, generate three referrals, and make two sales the next month as a result. Using those two sales as your basis for generating your next referrals, you'll end up with six leads, which translates to four sales. In other words, your sales *double* every month in this scenario. That means that by the sixth month, you've theoretically generated *thirty-two* sales for the seventh month, which is *way* more than enough business to keep you busy—especially when you consider that thirty-two-day months are pretty rare.

The point is that what I call "word-of-mouth" (or, to use the current buzzword, "networking") has the potential for putting more business in front of you than you know what to do with—and that's a nice problem to have to address.

There are, of course, other ways to establish yourself among professionals likely to use your services. One of the most popular for consultants over the years has been to join business, social, or special interest clubs. Again, you can use the term "networking" here, though the phrase is both overworked and slightly cynical in this context, as well. If it helps you, go ahead and "network" in these organizations. For my part, I "join" them and "meet" people. (How about those for buzzwords?)

The Rotary Club. The Kiwanis Club. The Chamber of Commerce. Whatever. If the group seems relevant to the economy of your community or tied in somehow to the business you'll be conducting, join it. Shake hands with people. Find out who does what. And tell whomever you're talking to what it is that you do!

Remember: You're not just meeting people to meet people. *You're trying to build a client base.* That doesn't mean that you have to give everyone you meet a full-fledged sales pitch. But you should be prepared to enter the group with an objective: to pass the word along that you are John Smith, you work in Anytown, and you offer consulting services to people who need help in such-and-such a business area. Make sure that the business card you circulate reinforces the specifics of those three simple facts, and you're ready to roll.

Try to become active in the group or groups you select. Understand the goals of the people you're meeting with. Wherever possible, find a way to pursue those goals that doesn't interfere with your other work. Your goal is to become *visible*, and hangers-on aren't usually the ones who stand out in any group.

It works. I promise. Pursue membership in the relevant groups and promote yourself consistently, discreetly, and confidently, and you *will* notice something happening. If the service you offer is a realistic one, and the people you're talking to are, as a group, likely to need that service, you'll find that after a while, the people you've introduced yourself to will call you back. They will ask you questions. They will suggest that you talk to their brother-in-law at ABC Company who's got a real problem you may be able to help solve.

In a way, it doesn't matter *how* you get your name out among potential clients—only that you do.

To illustrate the point, let me share a little story with you about a friend of mine whose primary market was a broad one, mid- and upper-level managers at large firms.

My friend had a bit of a professional dilemma. He ordered a box of business cards, but had the misfortune of selecting a "bargain basement" printing firm for the job. The result was that he got back five hundred business cards with his name, Smith, misspelled: Smoth.

He happened to be pondering the problem for the first time while he was riding through the financial district of the city on a municipal bus. He'd already arranged to get a credit for the business cards, but, being a thrifty kind of guy, he wondered if there wasn't some way to put the typo-ridden cards to work.

Then an idea struck him. There he was in the financial district, where a lot of his potential customers spent a good eight to twelve hours a day. There were the cards sitting on his lap in a little box. There were the customers, walking busily to their next appointment with somebody who wasn't him. And there, as though beckoning to be used creatively, was an opened window immediately to his right.

He pondered the intricacies of the litter problem in the city where he lived, and then weighed that against the potential for future economic development in the region in general and his business in particular. He threw caution to the wind and the cards out the window of the bus.

Now, I'm not advocating that you airlift your business cards by cargo plane and execute some kind of saturation bombing strategy over your city. But one of the things I am advocating is that you think of unique ways to build up your good reputation—and, more importantly, your name recognition—among potential clients. That's what my friend did. And I think the approach he took was a very creative one.

After all, that week, ten people called his office asking to speak with Mr. Smoth.

Word-of-Mouth: Speeches and Seminars

Of course, there is another, slightly more refined way to get across the message that you're a consultant worth consulting with: public appearances, lectures, and seminars.

Many people shy away from the very thought of giving a speech in public—not so much out of stage fright as out of a terror that they lack the authority to give advice on a subject publicly. I've got news for you: You're an expert.

Say it out loud: "I'm an expert."

Why are you an expert? Well, let me answer that question by posing another one. If you aren't an expert, what on earth are you doing attempting to charge people for your services? In your field—be it advertising campaign review, computer system evaluations, consumer motivation analysis, or funeral home promotion—*you are an expert*. If you don't agree with that, you can't be a consultant. It's as simple as that.

You must approach the question of public seminars and speeches—and, indeed, your whole practice as a consultant—from the point of view that you are an expert, that you're fantastic at what you do, that you're worth paying attention to. It's your business.

So, follow that train of thought. If you're fantastic, and if it's your business to be fantastic, you should be very interested in getting your message across to more than one person at a time. Find a vehicle that will allow you to speak in front of important organizations: The groups we discussed in the section above are a great place to start.

There are two very good reasons for doing this. The first is credibility. Conveniently enough, the more convincingly you get your message across in a speech or seminar setting, the more you become an expert. There's nothing that sets you apart from the pack more quickly than being accounted as a "noted lecturer" on a given subject.

You know your subject. You can lecture. Get someone to note you. Pretty soon there'll be a lot of people noting you. Then you'll be a "widely noted lecturer."

The second reason—and the one most directly related to your efforts to expand your client base—is that lecturing is a great way to meet people. And not just any people: people who stand a good chance of having an interest in your specialty and, hence, in your services. Many people (who are really looking for a reason to avoid giving lectures) ask themselves, how do I know that those kinds of people will really show up?

Who else is going to?

When I lecture and give seminars, I know that the people who attend are interested in the subject of sales training. My event has been publicized through the newsletter of the organization I'm working with. I've circulated flyers to my own personal contacts. I may even draft a press release and try to have it printed in one of the relevant trade journals.

All these efforts are targeted toward people who have an interest in the topic I'll be addressing. Those are the ones who'll show up. If they're interested in the topic, they *may* have a problem related to the sales staff in the company they work for. Solving those kinds of problems is *exactly* what I'm here for! Maybe I could talk to those sorts of people at intermission or after the program!

How do I *know* they're interested in sales training as a topic? Why don't I assume they're coming in expecting to take a dance class? Instinct.

The point is, giving lectures and seminars exposes you to the best possible audience *in the best possible setting* you can imagine. You're in command. You control the agenda. And you can highlight your knowledge of the topic in any way you see fit.

Go to the club or organization you've targeted. Say something along the lines of, "Look, I have expertise in analyzing the effectiveness of mechanical chicken pluckers. A lot of the members of your group are poultry people. What I'd like to set up is a program that would allow me to address some of the issues that are of real importance to the membership." Nine times out of ten the group will sponsor the event and help with promotion.

Do you charge admission or any kind of fee? Probably not at first, though if the group offers to pick up your transportation and preparatory costs, or to help you with a personal mailing, the world will probably spin a little more smoothly for you.

Even though there's a certain amount of risk involved—many people rate speaking in public as one of their very worst fears—lecturing and giving seminars remains an excellent way to generate leads. And once you've established yourself enough to begin charging realistic speaking fees, you'll find that this area of activity can provide you with some very attractive income opportunities as well.

At the conclusion of this book, you'll find an Appendix listing major organizations of interest to consultants. Many of these groups—as well as the far larger number of local and industry-specific organizations—are excellent resources for any number of activities related to speeches and seminars. Check out the resources in the Appendix, check your local business directories for smaller organizations that may be worth exploring, and get involved.

The Internet

I could write (and other people have written) entire books about the person-to-person networking potential of the Internet. For the purposes of this book, I'm limiting myself to a few remarks on two important topics: establishing your own World Wide Web site, and taking the initiative to connect with prospective clients through other cyberspace channels.

First, a few words about setting up your own Web site. Unless this is your own area of expertise, you should find someone who has a *demonstrated* record of performance in developing sites for businesses such as yours, as well as the references to back that record up. It took us five attempts to find the right team.

Yes, there are plenty of services that offer free or low-cost Web site development. The problem is that most of the sites they provide end up looking simplistic, incompetent, or a combination of the two. Image counts for a great deal on the

Internet. If your site is awkward-looking, unprofessional in conception, hard to navigate, or amateurish in execution, the problem will reflect on you, not on the "bargain" developer.

I'm not suggesting that you break the bank in order to develop a four-page Web site. I am suggesting, however, that you avoid signing up for the "free" and "discounted" offers a lot of fast-talking computer jockeys are hawking these days. In the twenty-first century, an attractive, professional-looking Web site is as essential as a business card or a phone number. Make sure the site you attach your name to says the right things about your practice, and make sure, too, that the site encourages visitors to contact you and makes it easy to do so. That's the whole point, right? You'd be surprised how many company Web sites there are out there with no "Contact us" button or equivalent. My bet is that most of these were designed by newcomers who charged little or nothing for their work—and still ended up costing their clients a great deal.

Do the research. Hunt down a Web site developer with a track record you can trust. Call the references. One good place to start your search is *www.expertcenter.net*, a sharp, intelligently designed site offering Web services and e-commerce specifically for speakers, consultants, and medium-size businesses. The company's own site is testimony to its ability to develop professional-looking material for consultants and speakers, and its database of useful articles and other resources is excellent. Further contact—including a check of previous customers and past jobs—might lead you to conclude that this organization can help you develop a Web presence for your practice. (Note: In addition to site development, the company also has a wide variety of promotional and networking tools, most of them free or modestly priced.)

If you're starting from scratch, expect to pay between $800 and $1,200 for a basic four-to-six page Web site (plus a modest monthly hosting fee). Be ready to promote your site both on-line and off. For starters, that means incorporating your Web site address and e-mail address on all business cards, stationery, and other promotional materials. For some excellent in-depth advice on promoting your site, visit *www.the1000.com* or *www.sotkin.com*. (And while you're at it, check out our site: *www.dei-sales.com*.)

When it comes to using existing Internet resources to promote yourself, your site, or your practice, you'll probably find that a certain amount of trial and error is necessary to identify the right forums. I've included a few of my favorites below. The challenge in isolating any Internet site for inclusion in a book like this is that the on-line landscape changes very quickly. In the brief listing that follows, I've selected resources that have shown some staying power and seem, as of this writing, likely to stick around for a number of years more. Use them as a starting point, and do a little surfing to develop a customized list of your own.

www.sixdegrees.com is the world's best personal connection site, period. Spend an hour and a half getting an understanding of how SixDegrees works (it's a little bit like that movie game involving the actor Kevin Bacon), and you'll find yourself coming back again and again to connect with new and old acquaintances. This is the ultimate virtual community. Do not fail to join. (It's free.)

www.mcni.com is the site for Management Consulting Network International. In addition to providing ample resources for members hoping to market their services, the site offers an article database, an invaluable set of links to relevant organizations, and much more.

www.imcusa.org is the superb site operated by the Institute of Management Consultants; it offers a wealth of resources to its members.

www.igpc.org is an information-rich site maintained by the International Guild of Professional Consultants. Well worth exploring.

www.kennedypub.com points you toward the publishers of *Consultants News* and other publications of interest.

www.hronline.com offers a wealth of news and resources of interest to those whose specialties relate to human resources; trainers, in particular, will want to use this site to subscribe to TRDEV-L, a rich source of news and leads.

www.aquent.com is a great marketing, networking, and information resource for "free agents"—independent professionals, including consultants. Check it out.

Finally, *Consultants*, an essential discussion group, is yours for the asking, and it's free. To subscribe, simply send the text "subscribe consultants" to the following address: *listproc@ listserv.oit.unc.edu.*

Mailings

There are two main types of mailings relevant to your consulting practice. The first is a *bulk mailing*; the second is what I call a *personalized mailing.*

If you're even considering a career in consulting, the chances are that you're in the middle of your earning years, that you're well educated, and that you are not unfamiliar with some success—or potential success—in the business world. Consequently, you, personally, are already a prime target for an avalanche of bulk mailings.

Bulk mailings are often referred to as "junk mail," and there's a reason for that. Think about it. How much time do *you* spend going over your daily "take" of coupons, impersonal sales pitches, and sweepstakes entry forms? If you're a busy working person, probably not too much.

One of the mistakes beginning consultants make in this area is that they expect an unrealistic return from bulk mailings. If they buy a list from a mailing house of, say, seven thousand names, their hopes will soar. An audience of seven thousand! Why, if a *fifth* of that, even a *tenth*, got back in touch right away, they would form the foundation for an incredible client base! What a start!

Here's the bad news. In most situations, a return of *one percent* is considered quite respectable on a bulk mailing. A really good mailing will often produce only a two percent response. So you're really talking about hundredths, not fifths or tenths.

What you're talking about, when you get right down to it, is a ninety-eight percent "no" in your *good case scenario*. And we haven't even talked about the problems you can encounter that cut into that precious two percent: outdated or inaccurate lists, delays by mailing houses over which you have no control, or problems with printers and typesetters. You should be prepared for all that when you undertake a bulk mailing, and you should be aware of the fact that there are definite risks involved.

Want to talk about risks? Recently, my office did a ten thousand piece mailing, publicizing an upcoming program. Care to take a guess at our total number of responses?

One.

That calculates out to *one one hundredth* of a percentage point. Can you understand how it is that I've managed, over time, to temper my enthusiasm for bulk mailings?

Believe me, these campaigns do have their place. A great many businesses have experienced tremendous success in this area. But I'm not convinced bulk mailings are the smartest marketing route for a beginning consultant. There are just too many variables, too great a chance that some design flaw or other technical element will adversely affect the results you get.

Rather than mail out ten thousand pieces at a clip, I'd rather see you—because yours is still, typically, a small business—mail out *five* pieces and follow each up by telephone.

Believe it or not, at the opening stages of your business, you're probably better off trying to chase down those five *qualified* referrals or contacts than you are blanketing your city with flyers. The fact of the matter is, until you've established a really solid reputation, you're more likely to close on the personalized letters.

After all, at this stage, what is it you really want? Suppose your wildest dreams come true and you're inundated with business that comes your way as a result of an incredibly successful bulk mailing. Do you really have the resources right now to satisfy a hundred, two hundred, or a thousand clients?

My bet is that what you're really looking for is more along the lines of five, ten, maybe fifteen people for whom you can do a *spectacular* job. That way, you can build up your reputation among the insiders in your chosen industry—and make more contacts later on. That way, you'll eventually end up not only with a larger client base, but with the resources to service it.

If you're thinking of combining the two methods—purchasing a commercial mailing list and attempting to contact each one individually by telephone—you should be aware of the fact that it's not the most cost-effective way to do things. Most list companies will have a minimum order requirement, necessitating that you purchase perhaps ten thousand contacts. Remember that yours is still a small operation! It will take you so long to get even a tenth of the way into the list that the bulk of what you've bought will quickly become outdated and more or less useless. (As a general rule, these lists become obsolete very quickly.) Why pay for a list if you'll never be able to use ninety percent of it?

Cold Calling

As the above discussion on mailings indicates, telephone marketing is an important component of your overall marketing plan, and should not be overlooked by any beginning consultant. As it happens, cold calling—which means prospecting for clients by calling people you've never spoken to before—represents your most cost-effective option when it comes to identifying those crucial early clients.

Why? Because, when you make cold calls, you are investing your *time*, not massive amounts of your money.

This is one of the reasons that effective cold calling, pursued carefully and consistently, is the best possible way to win new clients, build a contact network, and generate revenue-producing assignments. Cold calling can yield remarkable results—even in consulting practices with a serious shortage of marketing dollars!

Cold calling, however, is a challenging task. It will probably require a certain amount of mental preparation on your part, especially if you've never done sales work before. But the results are well worth the effort it will take you to prepare adequately.

What's the most difficult aspect of this marketing technique? Without a doubt, it's the fact that people who do cold calling hear the word "no" a lot. Coming to grips with that, refusing to take it personally, learning to deal with it, and, most importantly, *maintaining enthusiasm* in the face of "No, thanks" on the very next call—these are tasks that even seasoned salespeople sometimes find difficult to carry out consistently. But the best of them always figure out a way to deal with someone saying "no." And so can you.

Let's assume, for argument's sake, that you will make most of your presentations in person and that you will see most of your contracts signed as a direct result of that presentation. (It's a safe assumption; most consultants operate in this way.)

So where does cold calling come in? It's a tool that allows you to make the appointment in the first place. It's a process whereby you take the latest issue of, for instance, your industry's leading trade magazine, jot down the names and numbers of all the people who look as though they might be able to use your services, and then turn that "raw" data into a list of *qualified prospects* by making a series of telephone calls to determine each person's level of interest in your services.

Cold calling is such a crucial element in your initial marketing plans that I'm going to go into it in much greater depth than with the other methods that I've outlined.

Ratios—How to Monitor Your Progress

Let's start with that initial list of people who *might* be interested in your services. (By the way, there's a big difference between people who might be interested and people who are. As you may know, people who actually have expressed an active interest in at least talking about using your services are known as *prospects*; I call people who could be interested, but haven't been spoken to yet, *suspects*.) You sit down with a bunch of names written on a sheet of paper. The names could have come from any number of sources: referrals from friends, mailing lists of groups you've joined, industry publications, even the phone directory. Presumably the people you've identified stand a pretty good chance of belonging to your market base.

How does a suspect become a prospect? How does that list of names turn into appointments on your calendar? How do you turn stacks of research into people who actually want to hear proposals?

The first thing you have to do is realize that, just as in the case of mass mailings we discussed earlier, you're going to have a certain percentage of positive responses. But while you're cold calling, those positive responses are going to take the form of appointments, not sales. The idea, of course, is not to close the sale on the phone, but to identify those people most worth meeting—the prospects.

The most effective way to do that is to determine your own personal rate of success in determining the interest of the people on your list.

Let's say you have a list of one hundred people in front of you. If you call those one hundred people, how many do you think will actually pick up the telephone and say "hello"?

For argument's sake, let's say that five of the people on your list have phones that are continually busy, disconnected, or out of order. You can't get through to five of the one hundred no matter what you do. So you can expect to make ninety-five *dials*. And let's try to take a guess at how many of those dials will result in your actually speaking to a decision maker—someone who has the power to say, "You know what, that sounds like a great idea. Why don't you come down and talk to me about it and I'll see if it's something I want to go ahead with."

Note that I'm not asking how many times you could expect someone to *say* that—yet. All that's being discussed is the number of your dials that will end up *resulting in a discussion* with such a person.

How about half. Let's say that half of your dials—or forty-seven calls—will result in your actually reaching a decision maker. Let's say, right now, that out of a hundred leads, you can expect to make forty-seven *completed calls*.

A *dial* is when you dial the correct number, the phone rings, and somebody—not necessarily your suspect, but somebody—picks up the receiver and says "hello" and is, for that span of a few seconds, anyway, willing to talk to you. A *completed call* is when a call results in your speaking with a decision maker, regardless of what that decision maker has to say to you.

So, we started out with a hundred. Now we're down to forty-seven. Let's keep going. Of those forty-seven completed calls, how many do you think will result in the decision maker agreeing to a visit?

Forget for a moment exactly what words you'll use to set up that appointment. Let's just assume that you're engaged in a cordial, professional, polite conversation with a fellow businessperson about your consulting firm, and that you conclude that conversation with the suggestion that you drop by sometime and outline what you can do for the sus-pect's company. How many of those forty-seven calls do you think might result in a meeting you schedule with the deci-sion maker?

How about a little over one-third of them? Let's say it's thirteen; that sounds reasonable. And of those thirteen, it's probably a fair guess that one of your contacts will back out on you before the appointment time comes around, don't you think?

So what we're saying is that you can make thirteen *appointments*, and then go on twelve *visits*.

An *appointment* is when you get a decision maker to agree that you should stop by and discuss your consulting services. A *visit* is when that decision maker actually does sit down with you.

Here comes the important part. Of those twelve visits, how many will result in sales?

This may be a little difficult to gauge at this point, as you're probably still familiarizing yourself with your market base. But let's take a stab at it anyway and say that you can sell one-fifth of your appointments. That rounds off to something like two sales.

What we've done—very broadly, of course—is identify rough targets for you to shoot for in your cold calling. Those one hundred names you started out with could, if they represent a realistic cross section of your true market base, result in approximately two sales.

These ratios aren't simply picked out of thin air, either. They're the result of years of observation of real salespeople in the real world with real competition. Let's take a look at the progression once again:

Leads: 100

Dials: 95

Completed Calls: 47

Appointments: 13

Visits: 12

Sales: 2

The Nineteen "No" Answers

We can get even more specific with the goals that have been established above. Let's take a look at the three most important elements of our sales cycle: completed calls, visits, and sales.

The best salespeople will tell you that there are exact targets you should shoot for in each of these areas. Those targets conform to the cycle we just examined, but they're worth looking at on their own. Let's assume that for every twenty discussions you have with a decision maker, you make five eventual visits. For every five visits you make, assume you should close one sale.

20-5-1

(Completed Calls-Visits-Sales)

By this point, you're probably wondering exactly what all these targets and numbers have to do with real-life consulting. The answer is: plenty.

We talked a little earlier about the mental preparation that usually has to accompany any cold calling campaign. This preparation is particularly important for people who have limited sales experience, and most beginning consultants fall into that category. Having a good idea of your *overall sales cycle* is essential if you are to realize exactly the role rejection will play in your efforts to get your practice off the ground.

Take another look at the numbers. Twenty completed calls, five visits, and one sale. That's one "yes" compared to nineteen "noes."

It would be a wonderful world indeed if it were possible to buy some laser scanner that you could pass over your list of completed calls to single out that one-in-twenty sale. But technology does have its limits. You do have to make the twenty calls. You do have to go on the five visits. Otherwise you don't get the sale.

And remember, if you do get the nineteen "noes" before you hear a "yes"—you're doing *well!*

The point is this: Those nineteen "noes"—which will, at the outset, probably be quite discouraging to listen to—*are an integral part of the process of finding clients.*

When you run into people who tell you that there's absolutely no possibility of their ever using such a service, that it's a very busy day, that they wish you would just bug off—guess what? *You're doing your job perfectly! Things are going exactly according to plan!*

You've *got* to run into the nineteen "noes"—otherwise you'll never get to the one "yes." You can extrapolate this even further. When you dial a number that is disconnected, or reach a company that refuses to let you speak with the decision maker, that's *fantastic!* Because you know that you have to get those kinds of calls out of the way so you can reach your quota of completed calls!

Cold calling is a funnel-like arrangement. It starts out very big at the top (one hundred leads) and narrows down to a small point at the other end (two sales). *You cannot jump from the top of the funnel to the bottom without covering the distance in between. You will never be able to look at a list of one hundred suspects and generate one hundred sales.*

How Cold Calling Affects Your Business

Let me make the point once more—the numbers we've reviewed are absolutely crucial to your success as a consultant. They're targets—realistic targets, but ones you'll have to work to hit. And because, as you begin your practice, it's a solid bet that cold calling is going to be your primary marketing tool, it's imperative that you understand the no-nonsense, business survival implications of the numbers we've discussed.

You remember the "rollercoaster" that we discussed in an earlier chapter. That's the peaks-and-valleys graph that illustrates one of the central problems facing a beginning consultant—namely, that when you're working on assignments, you're not prospecting for new work, and when you're prospecting for new work, you're not getting paid.

That model takes on even more importance when you sit down to organize your marketing plans. You have no option but to make your prospecting time as productive as possible. You have no option but to ensure that your business continues to exist by serving customers continuously.

Bearing this in mind, ask yourself a question. What happens if, while you are prospecting, making your cold calls, you get fed up with the rejection and, consciously or unconsciously, don't make the twenty calls we talked about?

It's simple math. If you don't make the twenty calls, you won't make the five visits. And if you don't make the five visits, you won't have that one new assignment. And if you keep repeating the cycle, you won't have *any* assignments.

Every working day that I'm in my office, I make fifteen cold calls. No matter what. Maybe my business is bursting with assignments today. Maybe my schedule is an absolute madhouse today. Maybe I am positively *rolling* in clients—today. You'll still find me on the phone every morning I sit down at my desk, day in and day out, making the cold calls. Now, obviously, I don't make the calls in order to arrange work for today; I make the calls to make sure that I have someone to see two or three months from now!

As a matter of fact, if I *am* swamped with clients today, there's only one real reason for that. Guess what it is. *Two or three months ago, I was certain to make fifteen calls every day!* If I hadn't made my calls then, I would not have the business today.

Your Personal Sales Cycle

The numbers I've put forward aren't etched in stone, but they are targets. If you work effectively at your prospecting, you can probably establish your own standards. The most important thing is not that you march in lockstep with every other consultant trying to get a marketing plan off the ground, but that you understand your own effectiveness at turning suspects into sales. I call this process your *personal sales cycle*.

If, for instance, you know that you want to close more sales and you find that your ratio of completed calls to visits is less than it could be, you might concentrate on trying to make two or three extra cold calls every day and try to up the ultimate number of visits you make. Or you could focus on redeeming some opportunities you might be missing in the cold calls themselves, without increasing the actual number of calls made.

Your cycle will be unique. There's nothing wrong with that. The only real problem arises when you don't know what your cycle is, and expect the assignments to materialize out of thin air. They won't.

What most beginning consultants must do is appoint themselves sales manager. The sales manager monitors technique, approach, and execution, and makes sure, as the time-worn phrase has it, that "the numbers make it onto the board."

In my business, I have certain targets that I set for myself. I monitor my progress toward the goals, and if something seems to be getting in the way, I take time out and try to determine exactly what it is. Here are the targets that would be most important to my sales manager—me.

Suppose that, every day, I make fifteen cold calls: that's seventy-five a week. Over the course of the week, I try to speak to thirty-five decision makers. My goal is to turn those conversations into five appointments (which I may, of course, schedule for some weeks down the line). Out of every five appointments—my average for the week—I try to close one sale. If I keep at it consistently, that means, after a while, I'm generating a sale a week.

I take two weeks off for vacation every year. That means that, if I hit my targets, I generate fifty new sales every year. That's what my sales manager is looking for. If I don't come through, he doesn't let me go on vacation.

Of course, it's an ongoing process. The appointments I make this week are the visits I make two weeks from now. The ratios will go up and down slightly, no matter how consistent

I am on the phone. Interestingly enough, though, there is one element over which I have complete control: I can make my fifteen calls, every day, no matter what. Those cold calls are the foundation of the whole structure, and without them, I won't hit my numbers.

Let's suppose I decide that fifty sales is unrealistic. Instead, I need eighty over the course of the year. Because I know that I can maintain the ratios in my own cycle and increase the volume of work somewhat, all I have to do is schedule a slight increase in the cold calls. Let's say I call twenty people every day instead of fifteen.

I can make one hundred calls a week, keep the same ratio, and reach fifty decision makers. Out of those fifty discussions, over a week, I can probably schedule eight appointments. If I continue to close sales on about 20 percent of the visits over the year (which would now be about four hundred), I've got my eighty sales.

Of course, the new assignments aren't coming out of nowhere: I'm putting slightly more time in every day. I've increased the dimensions of everything that's happening in the cycle. But it should be apparent to you how important those *five extra calls*—representing perhaps ten or fifteen extra minutes every day—really are to my marketing plans, my yearly goals, and my practice as a whole.

Is Cold Calling "Drudge Work"?

Typically, beginning consultants shy away from cold calling because they consider it uninteresting, low-level work.

This is, potentially, a catastrophic strategic error. As we've learned, there are a number of other marketing techniques available, but none is as tailor-made to the beginning practice as cold calling. As for the "drudge factor," don't be too quick to dismiss those nineteen "noes" as worthless. If you're starting up a practice, you must know who your potential clients are; you must be familiar with the ins and outs of your market segment; and you must, must, *must* know *why people aren't deciding to give you assignments!*

If you think exposure to rejection is an unnecessary annoyance, think again. *You are your sales force.* Part of the job of a good sales force is to let the "top brass" know what is going wrong on the battlefield. If some new factor has turned your market upside down, you must find out about it immediately and make adjustments in your business. You can rely on industry publications and "scuttlebutt" for such information, but constant, intensive contact with potential clients is a far, far more reliable and immediate indicator. Part of the key to using cold calling as a research tool is recognizing that it need not be confrontational in nature. Even a "dead-end" call can provide you with crucial facts you would not otherwise have at your disposal.

Is Cold Calling a Waste of Your Valuable Time?

Another common objection to scheduling time for cold calling is the idea that consultants are professionals whose time is highly valued and should not be squandered on the telephone with people who probably aren't interested in talking about his or her practice.

That's true!

But that doesn't mean you shouldn't cold call! It means you should cold call *effectively!*

When you run into someone who tells you frankly (perhaps even sternly) that they have no use for the service you describe, and see no use for it at any time in the future, there's a secret technique you can use to maximize your effectiveness. What you do is say, "Thank you very much; have a nice day!" Then you hang up and go on to your next call.

That's a trade secret that only the most advanced sales trainers can pass along.

Yes, your time is valuable. That's why you don't spend all day arguing with someone. (By the way, there probably aren't as many flat-out, categorical rejections out there as you think.) We'll go into exhaustive detail about exactly how much your time is worth later on in the book. For now, we can address this objection most directly with a simple illustration.

If you're in demand, your time is worth quite a lot. If you are the most highly-respected, exclusive, and sought-after consultant in the field of, let's say, senior executive placement, you will probably command some staggering fees. How staggering? Who knows? Two hundred dollars an hour? Four hundred? Five hundred? More?

Most beginning consultants, however, don't fall into that category. So let's take a look at the other end of the spectrum. If you are unknown to the vast majority of your market; if you have not yet made a real name for yourself; if you are trying to open up a new field that no one's familiar with—guess what? At the beginning, your time, based on *existing market forces,* isn't worth much.

Chances are you're not sitting all the way at that end of the scale either. But the point should be clear. Unless you can depend on clients tracking you down and beating on your door in the middle of the night, prospecting in general and cold calling in particular is an excellent idea—one that should probably be included in your marketing plan.

Want to talk about productivity? The reality is that, for the vast majority of beginning consultants, cold calling is *phenomenally* productive time. If you don't make cold calls, then (eventually) nothing happens. You have no new clients and are utterly dependent on repeat business! That's not a solid marketing approach. If you do make cold calls, you get to keep running your practice! How much more productive can you get?

Is Cold Calling Impossible to Do if You Have No Sales Experience?

Many consultants find themselves unable to begin cold calling because of a perfectly natural human reaction: fear. They're hesitant—sometimes petrified—to pick up the phone and actually talk to "total strangers" about their practice, much less ask to schedule a meeting.

Fear is a very real part of sales, and it's an issue that even the best salespeople constantly confront. However, it can be conquered quite easily. All you have to do is take a deep breath, remember that you have to hear "no" a number of times in order to hear "yes"—and then plunge ahead.

Now, I'll grant that there are some people who have more aptitude for this type of work than others. That's why you'll find many practices constituted as partnerships; often one of the parties will handle the drafting of proposals and do the "real work," while the other will "just" line up customers. This is a popular, workable, and perfectly legitimate setup. (And by the way, if you don't consider lining up customers to be "real" work, you're in for a surprise.)

But I firmly believe that, if you plan on being a consultant, you'd better be able to discuss intelligently—with *anyone*—exactly what you do, whom you do it for, and why it's beneficial for a business to sit down with you and talk about it. Certainly that's no radical idea, is it? That if you plan on being a consultant you could expect to talk with someone at, for instance, a cocktail party, and mention why businesses should hire you for what you do?

That's all you have to do when you're cold calling!

Honest. There are only two differences. Firstly, of course, you're not at a cocktail party, you're on the telephone; and, secondly, you discuss the subject in sequence, with a number of different people. That is to say, you tell the person who you are, what you do, and why it can be beneficial to him or her, and you expect to do the same thing on a number of subsequent calls.

Maybe some of the calls will be encouraging as far as you're concerned; maybe some will be frustrating. That's not tremendously important, though. What's most important is that you *commit* to making the calls as part of your overall sales cycle. When one is over, you write down what happened, go to the next name on your list, and make the next call. You keep doing that until you've reached the number that's been set by your sales manager—you.

So, how do you do it? What do you say? What happens when they interrupt you? How do you know if they're interested? What happens when you do make a visit?

We'll tackle all these questions—and many more about the specifics of the sale—in the next chapter.

CHAPTER 4

The Anatomy of a Sale

What to Say on the Telephone

Do you remember that brief written summary you put together, the one that outlines what your consulting firm does? Take it out and look at it again.

That summary is going to form the foundation of your approach (or script). It's going to be an important tool. You'll use it to determine what exactly should be said on the telephone.

There are two things about cold calling that are important to keep in mind. One is that *you're not trying to close the sale over the telephone.* Trying to come away with a sale when you hang up the phone works phenomenally well for a lot of businesses. Consulting isn't one of them. There's too much money at stake, and the decision to hire a consultant is too strongly dependent on things like follow-through, chemistry, and even personal appearance.

What you want out of the cold call—and what you will ask for openly—is an appointment.

The second thing to bear in mind is that it's best to keep cold calls *nonconfrontational* in nature. You'll be wasting your time if you harangue people who have busy schedules just like you—and worse, you won't get any pertinent information out of them. So, as you formalize your approach, remember that

you're trying to initiate polite, professional contact, and determine whether it makes sense to get together in person to discuss what you do.

Right now, we're going to learn how to put together a
customized cold-call approach. The sole aim of this call is to
get you a face-to-face appointment. (Note: What follows is a
condensed summary of some of the techniques my company
has shared with some of the most prestigious firms in the
country, including Federal Express, Sprint, Aetna, Motorola,
and many others.)

Where do most people go wrong in cold calling? One
answer is that they decide that they must tell their contact, over
the phone, about everything they do, up to and including
internal technical processes of little or no interest to the person
on the other end of the line. Who cares?

You don't want to get a massive "product dump" when
you get a call from someone you don't know, do you? I
know I don't. Ask yourself: What is your main objective
when you receive an unsolicited sales call. Isn't it to get off
the telephone?

Let's be honest. Nobody leaves open a slot on the daily
planner for receiving cold calls. We're all too busy for that. So the
first thing we have to understand in developing our cold-calling
approach is *what the other person is thinking*. More likely than
not, the person who picks up the phone when we call is going
through a series of questions that sound something like this:

- Who is this person?
- Why is this person calling me?
- Is it important?
- What does this have to do with me getting my job done?

Well, the approach we're going to develop addresses all of
those questions directly, and makes three and only three direct

appeals for a face-to-face meeting. If those appeals don't result in an appointment, we're going to say "Thank you" and move on to our next call.

There's a very good reason you should give what I'm about to outline for you an honest try: It works. It gets you the appointment, which is the first step in developing the relationship.

What you're about to read has worked for small businesses, big businesses, middle-size businesses, and nonprofit organizations. It's worked for banks, for telecommunications companies, for insurance organizations, for scrappy little Internet startups, for computer-industry giants, and, yes, for consulting practices large and small.

So try it, exactly as it's laid out here. If it gets you the results you want, keep doing it. Don't tinker around with it; don't use only the parts that initially feel comfortable to you. Follow the steps exactly as I lay them out, and stick to the plan.

Spend half of your available time prospecting in this way— at least for the first year—and you will schedule plenty of meetings with prospective customers. That's right—the rule of thumb is that ten out of twenty business days should be devoted to prospecting activities in a beginning consulting practice. That means getting *very comfortable indeed* with the cold-calling approach you're about to learn.

Our objective is to get the appointment—nothing else. We're not trying to sell our services yet. When we make the call, our aim is simply to identify people willing to sit down with us and talk about what we do. Here's how we're going to make that happen.

The first step in the cold call is to get the person's attention. Do that by saying the person's name.

Good morning, Mr. Smith.

The second step allows you to identify yourself. Do this by following up with your name and your company's name, and provide a very brief summary of what you do. This step answers the question, "Who is this person?"

> *This is Carol Jones from Jones Consulting. I don't know whether or not you've heard of us, but we specialize in sales training for companies in the widget industry.*

The third step is to give a reason for the call, and to introduce a benefit statement. To do this, you should adapt the benefit you identified earlier in the book. This step answers the question, "What does this person want?" Notice the direct benefit that's outlined in the statement below.

> *The reason I'm calling you today specifically is so that we can set up an appointment to talk about how we increase total sales by helping salespeople set more appointments.*

The fourth step is optional, but I suggest you include it; it encourages the person you're talking to to offer a "yes" response, and it answers the questions, "Why is this call important?" and "What does this have to do with getting my job done?"

> *I'm sure that you, like a lot of the people we talk to, are interested in increasing sales.*

The fifth step is a direct request for an appointment *at a specific time*. Offer one time and one time only. The issue should be the *time* of the appointment, not whether or not the person will *grant* you an appointment.

> *What I'd like to do is set an appointment so we can get together and talk about this. Would next Tuesday at 3:00 P.M. work for you?*

Look at it again. Here's what it sounds like in sequence:

> *Good morning, Mr. Smith.*
>
> *This is Carol Jones from Jones Consulting. I don't know whether or not you've heard of us, but we specialize in sales training for companies in the widget industry.*
>
> *I'm sure that you, like a lot of the people we talk to, are interested in increasing sales.*
>
> *What I'd like to do is set an appointment so we can get together and talk about this. Would next Tuesday at 3:00 P.M. work for you?*

The point is not to memorize all the words you've just read, but to develop a script of your own that hits all the same points and accomplishes all the same things. *That's* the script you should practice until you can deliver it confidently and seamlessly. (A side note: Although there's a great deal of latitude in developing your own language for this script, you really should use "the reason I was calling you specifically" verbatim. It's a highly effective phrase that keeps momentum on your side.)

As I've said, you're going to use this approach to make up to three direct requests for an appointment, being sure to specify *one* date and time. Often, before you even get to your first request, your contact will interrupt you by saying something like this:

> *Carol, let me stop you right there—I have absolutely no interest in this.*

What do you say? Well, if you've been selling (and yes, that's what we're doing, selling!) for more than a week or so, you're not going to say, "Not interested? That's a new one! What will they think of next!" As a matter of fact, if you were training someone else to make cold calls, and you were giving advice on how to handle objections like "I'm not interested," my guess is that you'd probably be able to pass along some pretty good advice. You'd probably smile and say, "Hey, don't worry about it—that's what people said to me, too. And you know what, I even ended up selling to some of them!"

Well, if that's true—and for most consultants who've done any kind of engagement, or even worked in a related field, it is—then there's nothing wrong with saying that to Mr. Smith. Here's what it might sound like.

> Mr. Smith: *I'm going to stop you right there, Carol. We already have sales training. I have no need whatsoever for more sales training at this point in time.*
>
> You: *You know, Mr. Smith, other people in your industry have told me exactly the same thing before they had the chance to see how what we have to offer could complement what they were already doing. Let's get together. How's Wednesday at 2:00?*

This is an extremely effective turnaround. Practice it. You'll find that, once it becomes second nature to you, and once you instinctively ask for a *specific date and time* to meet with the person, you'll never want to change this technique. You'll have no difficulty setting up appointments with prospective clients—once you commit yourself to setting aside the time you need to make the calls.

A word of explanation is in order here. What you've just read is an rudimentary summary of some of the techniques on cold calling that I've shared with nearly half a million salespeople over the years. For a fuller discussion of the subject, including some very effective variations on the basic approach and a great deal more advice on handling objections during the cold call, see my book *Cold Calling Techniques (That Really Work!)*.

Other Cold-Calling Points to Keep in Mind

Here are some additional points to remember as you make your cold calls.

1. **Don't get discouraged.** Remember that rejection is part of the sales cycle.
2. **Don't overmail.** Typical mistakes in this area include: mailing four hundred pieces, then trying to follow up on all of them within three days; using "Would you like me to send you some information?" as a convenient way to get out of the conversation; or sending mail to unqualified or uninterested contacts. More often than not, requests for literature are usually polite ways of telling you that the contact doesn't really want to continue the conversation. The response I train salespeople to use when they encounter the "send literature" obstacle is your best bet: "Actually, I prefer not to send literature. Why don't we just get together instead—how's Tuesday at 2:00?"
3. **Don't interrupt—listen.** Nothing marks you out more quickly as pushy and hard to do business with than rudeness on the phone. Be brisk and professional, not antagonistic. Keep things in perspective. Don't take out frustrations on someone who has nothing to do with the way your day has gone.
4. **Ask for the appointment.** I'm repeating this point because it's so common for beginners to overlook it, and it's vitally important. Ask *directly* for the appointment.

Don't hem and haw or ask, "What's best for you?" Suggest *one* time and *one* date. Take the initiative and see what response comes back.

5. **Always leave a message.** Keep the message simple, informative, and short. Be sure to speak slowly when you leave your own contact information. For more information on the best strategies for dealing with receptionists and message systems, see *Cold Calling Techniques (That Really Work!)*.

6. **Stick with it.** Remember, 50 percent of your available time must be devoted to prospecting, at least in the first year. That should add up to ten full business days at the end of the month. Schedule this time with yourself, and keep that commitment.

7. **Don't forget that you're talking to another businessperson.** Your contact has a to-do list to keep up with, too. Respect the person's time and attention. Don't get rattled. Use the call as an opportunity to display how you'd handle pressure on the job.

When Should You Make Your Calls?

As your business grows, you're going to have to find some creative ways to maintain your prospecting activity.

Consider, for instance, the following situation: Your first few days of cold calling give you two appointments, both scheduled on the same day. One is scheduled for ten o'clock; another is scheduled for one in the afternoon. Once you leave for that first appointment, guess what? Your whole day is pretty much shot.

Assume that both appointments go well. That means the ten o'clock appointment goes until twelve, and the one o'clock appointment goes until three. There may be only four scheduled hours there, but you've got a lot to do that doesn't usually make it onto the schedule. For one thing, you have to get to the prospect's office—early, of course. You have to leave some time to battle the traffic, both to and from the facilities. And at some point, you'll want to take, say, half an hour or an hour alone to jot down notes about the key points from each of the meetings.

So what's the problem?

Well, when do you do your daily prospecting? During your lunch break? That shows initiative, of course, but it may not be the smartest way to go if it means that you walk into your one o'clock appointment hungry and distracted.

So there's a challenge here. I'm not going to try to set your schedule for you, but I will tell you this: You can reach a lot of decision makers on the phone between eight and nine in the morning and after five o'clock in the evening. Those two periods are prime cold-calling time for me, and they certainly should be for someone who's trying to get a consulting practice off the ground. These two stretches of time are when a lot—not all, but a lot—of the real movers and shakers get their best work done. Many of them answer their own phones during these hours. If you're trying to figure out the best way to get your cold calling hours in for the day, you should definitely be making use of these two time slots.

That having been said, I should note too that consultants, to a much greater degree than many other members of the workforce, must be extraordinarily sensitive to how and when things are scheduled. The best consultants are demons for showing up on time, voracious about making sure everything on the list gets done, and relentless in their efforts to squeeze the most out of every working day. You're going to be one of the best consultants, right? That means you have to be schedule-crazy, too.

There are a great many instances, of course, where schedules will be thrown off balance. If you get your first assignment on the condition that you work with the client for five straight, full days, your commitment to spend, say, every morning from nine to twelve on marketing may have to be adjusted somewhat. Adjust. Feel free. But make the time up later. Remember the rollercoaster.

Remember that your overall goal is to shorten those deadly cycles that career between "no prospects" and "no money"— and to do it in a way that allows you to maintain a good working relationship with your clients. It's tough. There's no doubt about it. But it can be done. And it should be done by the best possible representative of your business—you.

Keep a diary—in addition to a schedule. Keep track of where every minute of your time is going, what your own personal ratio of marketing-to-servicing is. Monitor yourself constantly, at least for the first year of your business. If you do, you'll be keeping track of your most important asset, and you'll be able to make informed decisions on the crucial issue of how much time you should devote to your prospecting.

The Four Steps of the Sale

Having discussed the ins and outs of identifying prospects in some detail, we're ready, finally, to take a look at what happens when you walk in the door.

While there are thousands of different directions a consultant can take in serving clients, the actual pattern of a sale, from the first appointment to the decision to engage your services, is basically similar from practice to practice.

There are four main steps. We'll look now at each one in detail.

Step One: Qualifying

You've spoken with the prospect on the phone. Things look good. You set up an appointment.

Your first meeting is the *qualifying* step. Granted, the prospect is going to be taking a very close look at you to see if your services meet his or her needs. But, more importantly from your point of view, *you are evaluating the prospect as well.*

Is this the kind of person you can—and want to—do business with? Do you feel good about the organization? Can you in fact solve the problem you're likely to be asked to solve? Are you sure you know whom you'll really be reporting to? Are you confident that you'll actually get paid?

That last question is one that is, unfortunately, often given less attention than it deserves. Especially in the early going, the temptation will be to take any assignment, in an effort to build your reputation in a given field. There's really nothing wrong with doing volunteer work—and I'm not being at all sarcastic when I say that. Working for community organizations or other groups on a complimentary or reduced-fee basis is a good way to make a name for yourself. But working for a profit-making venture and getting stiffed is not the way to rise in the world. Know what you're getting into.

Qualifying is the step that precedes everything else in your face-to-face work with a prospect. You must determine that *you* think the project is worth pursuing. The prospect must pass *your* audition.

If I walk into an office and see nothing but danger signs, I don't do the project. What *is* a danger sign? That's something that will vary from practice to practice. What I look for might incorporate any number of problems: The sales staff might be smaller than the ones I ordinarily train; I might not like the way the firm runs its business; I could anticipate a major personality conflict with the person who'll be working with me; I might not have a good feeling about my receiving payment in the period of time I'm accustomed to. In all of these situations, I would take a pass on the assignment.

It's nothing personal. It doesn't mean I'm rude to the person I'm speaking with. All it means is that the job isn't right for me. After all, the whole idea is to take assignments on which you can deliver superior results, right? If the environment, the people, or the money is wrong, there's very little chance that the job will come out right.

Step Two: Interviewing

This is where you find out what the individual you've contacted is doing now and hoping to accomplish in the future. You do this in order to determine what you are going to say in your presentation.

I say "individual" rather than "company" for a good reason. From this point onward, it's very important to remember that you're not dealing with the ABC Company; you're dealing with Jane Brown, who works there and who may be able to do what she does better if she works with you. Your relationship with the prospect must reflect a commitment to make even difficult goals attainable.

Among the questions you should ask your prospect during the interviewing portion of your meeting are these:

What have you done in the past to deal with this problem?
Have you ever used this type of service before?
If so, what happened?
Are you doing anything at present to solve this problem?
What are your future plans in this area?

Obviously, it's important for you to learn the answers to these questions. Asking them will probably give you a lot of valuable background information on the situation you're likely to inherit. In addition, if a previous consultant has tried and failed to work things out, you'd better know what techniques were used, so you can keep from making the same mistakes! And knowing what the contact has planned for the future gives you an idea of both what your proposal should look like at its completion, and whether there's a possibility of working with this firm later on.

At this stage all you are is a gatherer of information. You have not yet committed to the assignment. You *can't* commit to the assignment until you make your proposal, and you can't make your proposal without data. So your objective during the interviewing stage is to gather information. Nothing else.

Don't give advice of any sort during the interview stage. In my training programs, I warn people that they must be prepared to spend at least 75 percent of the sales-process time in the interview step. It is absolutely essential that you obtain all the information you can during this phase, and the best way to do that is to ask questions about the *past,* the *present,* and the *future*—as well as appropriate *how* and *why* questions. What's more, before you can move forward to the next step, you must *verify* that your information is accurate. My favorite way to do that is with a *preliminary* proposal or outline. This is a short summary of what a formal proposal might incorporate. Basically, it's a short document that says, "I am not a proposal." The aim is to get the prospect to offer detailed corrections to this preliminary draft and give you feedback you can incorporate verbatim in your formal presentation.

Of course, the interview stage may well require more than one visit. How should you ask for the second visit? Well, you'll certainly accelerate your sales cycle if you ask to schedule your follow-up visit *at the conclusion of your first meeting.* (A great reason for scheduling that follow-up meeting is to review your preliminary proposal with the prospect.)

Step Three: Presentation

Remember our old friends, *features, benefit,* and *proof?* They make important appearances at this stage.

We'll look in detail at the specifics of how to assemble the formal proposal in a later chapter. For now, though, be prepared to produce a written document you feel comfortable discussing in depth that:

Incorporates the knowledge you gained during the interview,
Outlines what you plan to do to solve the problem,
Highlights the features of your service,
Forecasts the ultimate benefit of your service—*stated, if at all possible, in dollar terms,*
Reinforces your image as a competent problem solver by providing ample proof.

When the right moment finally rolls around, this is what you'll submit to your contact in writing. This is what you'll summarize orally. This is what will get you—or lose you—the job.

The presentation is the put-up-or-shut-up section of the sale. If you don't have a realistic solution to the problem you've identified—or if you can't explain that solution in a way that your prospect will understand—you're out of the running.

Just as you did in the cold-calling process, you're likely to run into some objections at this point. The same basic techniques apply in dealing with them. Make sure that the prospect knows that *you understand* the objection by repeating it to him or her. Show why the client's fears aren't going to come to pass. Show why your service is the best move from a financial viewpoint—highlight *savings* to the company or *benefits* to the company's customers. Wherever possible, *cite relevant examples* from your previous work with other clients.

(If you have zero experience with other clients, you have a tough job ahead of you. Your best bet is to highlight elements of your previous work background that mesh well with the solution you're proposing, or, as I mentioned earlier, draw the client's attention to volunteer or less-than-full-fee work you may have completed for a community group or similar organization.)

Finally, you'll move on to the fourth step, which may or may not take place at the same meeting you use to submit your proposal and outline its contents in person. The final step of the sale is the *close*.

Step Four: Closing

"That's our proposal. It makes sense to me . . . What do you think?"

That's a perfectly reasonable question to ask, don't you think? You've put all this work into researching the client; taking a good, long look at the problem; and coming up with a realistic, cost-effective recommendation. Why would you spend all that time if you didn't want to *help* the client by getting to work?

When you close the sale, you're going to *ask* to do the job in the same way you asked for the appointment: *openly*. And your doing that is not inherently aggressive, pushy, or inconsiderate. It's *supremely* considerate. You want to help out the client and solve the problem as quickly and as efficiently as possible. So you say something straightforward.

The "makes sense to me" close is easy to remember, easy to execute, and extremely effective. Look at it again: "This is what we do. This is how we charge. Are there any other questions I can answer for you about the proposal? Okay. Well—it makes sense to me . . . what do you think?"

And then—here's the real trick—you *wait for an answer*. As we learned a little earlier, your goal is to close one sale out of every five visits. If you've made a strong proposal, identified something you can help the person to do better, and proposed a workable, affordable plan, it should come as no surprise to you to hear someone answer "Sure!" one time out of five.

The beauty of the "makes sense to me" close (beyond the fact that it doesn't try to play games with the other person) is that it positions you perfectly to find out *why* your proposal doesn't make sense if some obstacle remains. This close encourages the other person to tell you exactly what the problem is—and leaves you in a great position to revise your approach. If things aren't clicking, just remember your aim is to close on one out of five, not five out of five, which is pretty close to impossible. Keep your head up. Tell the prospect you plan to check back in a month or so to see what the company is doing at that point in time. Four to six weeks later, get back in touch with the contact. (Actually, you should also be sure to check in this way upon the completion of an assignment for a client. Such informal calls are the key to a consultant's repeat business.)

The Prospect Management System

I want to share a tool that will help you hit your revenue goals and manage your selling activity. It's called the Prospect Management System.

A word of warning: The system requires that you classify your contacts accurately and consistently. It shows you exactly where every current lead is, and it identifies precisely what you have to do to develop the income you need to grow your business.

Here's how the system works. For each active contact, you will write down the company name, the next scheduled appointment (or other next step), the estimated value of the sale (that's very important for forecasting purposes), and any other relevant information. Then you'll use a similar process to identify inactive contacts, such as companies you haven't been able to meet with yet, or people who told you to "call back in six months." You can use a deck of small index cards for this task, or, if you prefer, you can get a set of easy-to-store cards and a small board to keep track of them by contacting D.E.I. Management Group. (The number to call is 1-800-224-2140; you can also visit us on the Web at *www.dei-sales.com*.)

Whatever system you use, once you've identified both your active and inactive contacts, make sure each card includes the company name, your contact's name, and the date of your last discussion. Your next job is to place each and every one of those contacts into one of six specific categories. Get a large bulletin board and divide it into six vertical columns, one for each category. These categories will help you develop a "snapshot" of the business you're currently developing. But you must classify accurately in the first place for the system to work!

This classification step is extremely important, because it allows you to see exactly what's "on the horizon" for each card, and to evaluate how many contacts are in each category. In this section I'm going to develop the classification system with you, so be sure you have all your leads and appointments handy.

Each of the categories in the system has a specific set of criteria for inclusion. As I've mentioned, every single contact you can identify should get a card; the cards should go into one of six columns. The columns are labeled as follows:

O   FA   #1 (25%)   #2 (50%)   #3 (90%)   C

What do the labels mean? Well, reading from left to right, we have Opportunities, First Appointments, the #1 column (representing a 25% chance of closing), the #2 column (representing a

50% chance of closing), and the #3 column (representing a 90% probability of closing). The last column is for Closed business.

Please understand that each column does *not* represent a week or month, but the probability of a sale based on predetermined criteria. Although dates do play a very important role for each individual card, the categories themselves reflect the *status* of your relationship with the contact, not the amount of time you've spent with a person.

So what do each of the columns represent? Well, you may have already guessed that the Opportunities column on the far left-hand side is meant for contacts that we *may* turn into active prospects at some point in the future. And the Closed column, on the far right, represents signed contracts we've received. So, it's clear what we're doing: The further to the right the card is placed, the higher the quality of the contact— the higher the probability you're actually going to get income from it.

In order to give you the best possible understanding of the criteria that operate in each column, I want to start with the most important column, the one that is the heart of the whole board. As it turns out, the first and most important column to understand is the #2 column, which represents prospects that have a 50 percent probability of closing.

At this point, you may well be asking yourself—how do you know that you have a 50/50 chance of closing any given sale? What has to be true of prospects that go into this column? Well, the first thing is that you have to have held your initial meeting with your prospect. If you sell your consulting services through face-to-face appointments, and you have not yet met with a certain person, than obviously that lead does not represent a 50 percent probability of closing.

What else? Well, if you've gone on the first meeting, but the person has refused to schedule a follow-up meeting with you, clearly that's not a 50 percent prospect, either. We define prospects as people who are *actively* discussing the possibility of doing business with us. If there is no commitment to do that, we're not looking at a real prospect.

On the other hand, if you have had your first meeting, and that meeting has resulted in a second meeting, and you're coming back to make a presentation, then you *do* have something. Typically, this is the profile of the contact we place in the #2 (50%) column. The presentation has either already been made, or it's imminent. So when you make the presentation (that is, you show your prospect what it is that you are proposing that they do) assume that you have a 50/50 chance of closing that sale.

But . . . notice what goes into the definition of "a presentation"! For you to place a card in the #2 column, you must be discussing real dollars, with a real timetable, *and talking to the right person* within the target organization. What's more, we're going to assume that you're not making this presentation for your health—you have a real expectation of closing the sale.

Here, then, are the criteria for a prospect that we place in the all-important #2 (50%) column:

- First appointment has taken place
- Second appointment scheduled (or has already taken place)
- Real expectation of closing the sale
- Presenting to the right person (the decision maker), and discussing real dollars and a real timetable with that person

Admittedly, those are tough standards, but applying them regularly to determine who should go into the 50 percent column is what makes the entire Prospect Management system work.

Take a moment now to look over your appointment book or list of leads. Identify all the prospects that fit these 50 percent criteria. Make sure the cards include all the relevant information, and place the appropriate cards in the #2 (50%) column.

Next, let's go on to the #1 (25%) column.

With these prospects, you've already met with someone and, as a result of that meeting, you believe that you have a one in four chance of closing a sale. There's a "next step" of some form in place. So if you've met with the prospect for the first time, and it was a productive meeting, and you've set up the second meeting, then that prospect should go into the #1 column. If, however, you've set up the second meeting *in order to make the presentation,* then that card should go into the #2 column.

What, you may ask, is the difference between the #1 column and the #2 column in such a case? All the difference in the world. Remember that 75 percent of our time in the sales process should be spent *gathering information.* When a card is still in the #1 column, it means you are still collecting information in order to get to the #2 column so you can make your presentation.

In other words, the #1 column is for prospects that you've met with for the first time. You have a real appointment to go back to see them again, and you are still looking to get enough information to make the presentation and advance the card to the #2 column. The 25% column is for those people you have met with initially or who are interested in your product, *and* who have given you a second appointment—but who still have not given you enough information for you to make your proposal. Therefore, your objective in this column will be to get the right information, so you can make the proposal and advance the card from the #1 column to the #2 column.

Here are the criteria for the #2 (25%) column:

- Have already had first appointment
- Have scheduled a next step to gain information

Take a moment now to identify all the people who should go into your #1 (25%) column. Place the cards in the correct row before you read any further.

Let's go next to the #3 column. This is for people who have given you a credible verbal agreement to work with you. The #3 column is the closest that you can get to closing the sale without having a firm contract in hand.

We like to say that the #3 column is for "C.O.D." prospects. (That stands for "Contract on Desk.") If the person has the contract on his or her desk, and we have a reasonable expectation that that contract's going to be signed, then the prospect should be in the #3 (90%) column. If there is no contract on the desk and you *do not* have a reasonable expectation that it's going to close, the prospect should not be in the 90% column. (It should probably be in the #2 column, but before you place it there, doublecheck to be sure all the criteria are in place.)

Here are the criteria for the #3 (90%) column:

- Verbal agreement based on proposal
- Contract on desk

Take a moment now and put all the cards that meet these criteria in the #3 (90%) column.

What we've just seen are the three active prospect categories. Let's go now to the scheduled first appointment (FA) column. This *isn't* an active prospect category. Why not? Well, the person has not yet met with you. He or she has only agreed to do so—and sometimes those meetings do fall through.

The criteria here should be pretty obvious. In this column, there are only scheduled first appointments with companies or people you have not met yet. Scheduled first appointments (FAs) are *only* those upcoming appointments with a specific date, place, and time. Let's say you have an appointment to see John Smith two weeks from now, or a week from now, or tomorrow morning. That card would go into the FA column.

Here are the criteria for inclusion in the FA column:

• Scheduled first meeting at some point in the future
• Specific date, place, and time

Take a moment and look through your appointment book and put into the FA column all of your scheduled first appointments that you now have with people you have not met yet.

Now let's talk in more detail about the far left-hand column, which is labeled O for Opportunities. This column really is the softest column of them all. That is, it consists entirely of people *you want to see*. So the only meaningful criterion is that you hope to connect with this company or this person at some point in the future.

Remember, your objective in selling is always to advance the sale. That is, you want to go from an opportunity to a first appointment. You want to get from the FA column to 25%. You want to move from 25% to 50%. You want to win a verbal agreement. Finally you want to receive a signed contract. Therefore, your aim is to put into your Opportunity column all those people with whom you have not yet scheduled a first meeting. Your objective here is to start the process by getting from the Opportunity column to the scheduled appointment. The best way to do that is by calling the person and asking for a meeting!

Requirement for the opportunity column:

- You want to meet with the person, but have not yet scheduled an FA

Your column could be many times the length of the other columns; in practice, you should probably be working on ten or so opportunities at any given time.

Now that you understand what the columns are for, let's look at how you can use the board to diagnose your own sales activity. The visual information you get from the proportions of the various columns can be absolutely invaluable. Look at your board. What are the column lengths?

Let's say that when you completed this exercise you realized you had more in the #2 column than you had in the #3 column, and virtually nothing in the #1 column.

O	FA	#1 (25%)	#2 (50%)	#3 (90%)	C
O	O	O	O	O	
O	O		O	O	
O	O		O	O	
O	O		O	O	
O	O		O		
O	O		O		
O			O		
O			O		
O			O		

Well, you certainly have a high expectation of making sales now and a lot of things pending, but it will be obvious to you that there's a problem. Let's say your sales cycle is eight weeks. That means you have no sales eight weeks from now because the #1 column, which will produce your sales eight weeks from now, doesn't have enough prospects! You have to schedule more first appointments, and you have to start doing so right away!

In the ideal case, the #3 column will be shorter than the #2 column, which will be shorter than the #1 column, which will be shorter than the First Appointments column. That is to say, because cards are constantly dropping out, the best board formation possible will give you enough first appointments to convert to sales in the far right-hand column.

O	FA	#1 (25%)	#2 (50%)	#3 (90%)	C
O	O	O	O	O	O
O	O	O	O	O	
O	O	O	O	O	
O	O	O	O		
O	O	O	O		
O	O	O	O		
O	O	O	O		
O	O	O			
O	O	O			
O	O	O			

First appointments really do drive the whole process—which is why you must build your schedule around your prospecting activities. From that point of view, the system is an excellent time management tool; it shows you instantly when there are gaps and imbalances in your daily prospecting activity.

In the same way, the Prospect Management System shows you when your sales efforts are out of balance in the longer term. If you notice that a card hasn't moved for four or five weeks, you'll know right away that it needs to be reclassified as an opportunity. That's why the dating of cards is so very important; the system is dynamic, and anything that sits still for long is highly unlikely to be an active prospect. By looking at the dates on the cards, you can see very quickly whether or not the prospects on your board are in keeping with your normal sales cycle. If your sales cycle is ninety days, the longest you will have a card on your board is ninety days. After that point, the odds are that it will not be on your board. You will have either closed the sale or the card will have been moved back into the O column. (It's a fact of sales life that the longer a series of discussions with a prospect exceeds your normal sales cycle, the less likely that prospect is to close.)

As you evaluate the individual cards in the Prospect Management System, the first question to ask yourself is, "When am I going back to see this person?" If you cannot answer this question, the odds are that you do not have a real prospect. Such a card should be placed in the O column. Suppose there's someone in the #1 column you met with two or three weeks ago who said he was very interested in working with you. At that point, you said, "That's great; I'd like to come back next Tuesday at 2:00," but your contact said, "No, call me next week instead." Now you've called him three, four, five, or six times, and he is still not taking your call. You have no appointment; you have no prospect. The card should be removed and put in the O column.

Or let's say you're trying to reach somebody who was in the #2 column. You had three or four good meetings, and then you went in and gave your contact a proposal. You were talking about real dollars, you had a real timetable, and you were sure your contact was the right person to talk to. As a result, you honestly thought that proposal was going to close. You now call your contact back. One week goes by without a return call. Two weeks. Three weeks. Four weeks. Five weeks. Six weeks. Seven weeks—and she hasn't taken your call! Do you really think that card still belongs in the 50% column? Of course not. Well, is it a 25% prospect? Unfortunately, because she hasn't even taken your call, there's no next step at all. It's just an opportunity.

Another important question to ask is, "Do I know what they are doing now?" In other words, when you meet with this contact, do you understand what it is he is trying to accomplish—and does what you offer help him accomplish that? If not, the odds are that you're not going to make a sale. This is a vitally important point to bear in mind throughout the sales process. **Successful selling means asking people what they do, how they do it, when they do it, where they do it, why they do it, who they do it with—and then helping them do that better!**

Finally, as you evaluate your cards, you must ask yourself, "What am I going to do to move the sale forward when I go back?" That is to say, what steps are you going to take to advance the sale? How are you going to move the relationship from one column to the next? If you don't have a strategy for moving the sale forward, then you probably will not make much headway with the prospect.

Don't Kid Yourself!

Let me repeat a key point. The Prospect Management System needs accurate information in order to deliver accurate results. If you can't make realistic assessments of prospects and opportunities by checking them against the criteria you've just learned, you're deluding yourself (and wasting your time) when you write out the cards. If you have a board full of "prospects" that have no real likelihood of closing, that you have no appointment to go back to, or that you haven't even seen yet, there's no point even trying to use the system.

Typically, after evaluating their prospects honestly, people in our training seminars get a very glum look in their eyes. Actually, that's a very good sign. If, after doing this exercise, you find that you're uncomfortable with what your board looks like, congratulations. You now know what needs fixing. If you don't have enough cards in the #1 column, then you realize what your objective is: to get enough scheduled appointments to increase #1 column to the level where it needs to be. If you realize that you do not have enough first appointments, then you know what you need to do: Get the opportunities that will give you the appointments, or refine your cold calling approach. If you're noticing that many of your prospects seem to be drying up after you give a proposal—that is, most of the proposals do not lead to a close—then the odds are good that you're not getting enough information before moving the cards to the #2 column (50%). You may need to rethink the questions that you're asking.

You should know about problems like these *before* they become crises. Please do bear in mind, however, that in order to use the Prospect Management System as a diagnostic tool in this way, you have to be ruthlessly honest when classifying your contacts!

Once you learn to keep your assessments accurate, you'll find that you can also use the board to anticipate revenue. Estimate the dollar value of each card. Take all the prospects in the #1 column and figure out what 25 percent of the income would be from that column. Then take the cards from the #2 column and figure out what 50 percent of the income from this column would be. Finally, take the #3 column and figure out what 90 percent of the income from that column would represent to you. Add those three numbers together and you will have a realistic projection of what it is you expect to do based upon what's on the board now.

If that's not an aid to planning and forecasting activity in your consulting business, nothing is!

The Assignment's Cycle

We'll be discussing the complicated subjects of evaluating what a job is worth—and how much your time is worth—in a subsequent chapter. For now, though, you should take a look at the mechanics of exactly how you get paid for your services, and what you should expect to charge before even beginning work.

Many beginning consultants are so ecstatic about actually getting an assignment that they pay little or no attention to the billing arrangements. This is a mistake that, if repeated, will result in your not being a consultant for very long.

Let's take a look at the actual time frame that accompanies an "easy" sale (if there is such a thing) and the financial implications of letting your invoice for services rendered sit in the company's accounts payable bin until company policy dictates that you be sent a check.

November first. You make your first contact with the company in question through a cold call. You set up an appointment for one week later—November eighth.

November eighth. Your first interview with the contact. Green lights seem to be flashing, so you schedule another meeting to make your proposal.

November fifteenth. The presentation and close are so smooth you can't believe it. Your client is ecstatic about the idea of using you. You agree to begin work the following week.

November twenty-second. You show up and make your tour around the office, gathering all the necessary manuals, meeting the contact's subordinates, identifying the people who'll have to be retrained or supervised under different conditions. You get everything you need, go back home, and, looking everything over, determine that your initial estimate of one month to complete the job is probably about right.

December twenty-second. You finish the job. You drop by the office as scheduled to show the affected people what their new work arrangement looks like. Surprise! Everyone's dancing around—it's the company Christmas party: Bad time to start turning the world upside down. Your contact asks if you can come back after New Year's Day; that way everybody can start with a clean slate. You mark it down on your calendar.

January third. Everything goes smoothly. Two days of discussions with the top people at the company, and your new system is running perfectly. You've performed fantastically, met the deadline, kept friction to a minimum, and generally exceeded everyone's expectations. You hand your contact your invoice: The total due is twelve thousand dollars. You remember the nasty notes you've been getting recently from your landlord and the phone company. Good thing this job came along, you say to yourself; this fee couldn't come at a better time.

January twelfth. No word from on high: The invoice is still outstanding. Probably some accounting problem. You phone your contact at the company and mention tactfully that you haven't received payment. Is there a problem? Someone will look into it, says your (apparently very busy) contact. It should be settled by next week. If not, give a call back.

January twentieth. Bad news. You've had to go into your savings to pay the bills. You call the company again. Your contact has the story now: It turns out that all their bills are paid within ninety days of receipt; you submitted yours on, let's see, the third of January, so it looks like early April right now. Is there a problem with that?

April second. After weeks of frustrating (and useless) cajoling and lobbying, you get a check for twelve thousand dollars. It has been a full *five months* since you first started *your* work on this project.

Payment Terms

The scenario I've outlined above is, believe me, not uncommon. Because you're a small businessperson, with the attendant small business cash constraints, you simply cannot afford to operate on the terms most firms employ in paying their bills.

It's obviously a terrible idea to talk about payment terms before you've closed the sale. However, once you know you've landed the assignment, you should be certain to protect yourself, and try to establish the most workable terms possible.

You should ask for 25 percent of your estimated final fee on agreement—*before you do any work at all.*

You should ask for 50 percent more of your estimated final fee at a mutually determined point of the project, typically one that represents a point of around three-quarters of the total work you've scheduled.

You should ask for an agreement that your remaining balance be paid to you within *ten days* of your completion of the job.

These are tough terms. There's a very good chance you either won't get your client to agree to them, or won't be able to locate clients who consistently adhere to them. Nevertheless, you should think seriously about using these standards as a starting point before you do business with any client. The alternative, waiting up to four months before you see a cent for your efforts, is not a happy one, and may well drive you right out of business.

The Moral of the Story

It will probably come as no surprise to you that the ultimate message underlying this chapter is:

Prospect, prospect, prospect.

You have to have a number of potential assignments in the "pipeline" at all times. You have to be prepared for things going wrong, payments being delayed, appointments being missed, contacts who love you being transferred to another city. These things happen. There's no way to anticipate all of them.

What can you do?

Keep your appointment book occupied. That way, when the one unbelievable lead that's going to put you on top suddenly turns ice cold—you're covered. When you learn that your client's busy season ends abruptly on the first of January and he won't need to talk to you for another six months, thank you very much—you're covered. When the President of Umpty-Ump tells your contact, the Vice President of Umpty-Ump, that budgets are being tightened and all "nonessential" programs must be scrapped, now, by the end of business today—you're covered.

Don't let landing one assignment fool you.

One assignment can evaporate in the blink of an eye, no matter how promising it looks right now. Do yourself a favor. Do the prospecting.

CHAPTER 5

What Are You Worth?

The Bottom Line

We've examined, up to this point: who you are as a consultant, who you're going to sell to, and how you're going to market your services. Now it's time to discuss the question that is, for many beginning consultants, the most important issue of all: How much should you charge?

Presumably, making money was a major motivation in your decision to get into consulting. As you probably know, turning a profit depends to a large extent not only on your strategies, but also on the conditions in which you work. By conditions I mean not only the state of your market base, but also the surroundings and supplies you need in order to get the job done.

Your overhead costs—the amount of money you need for the nuts-and-bolts matters of staying in business, including paying rent, mailing letters, having a telephone to answer, and so forth—are going to carry a great deal of weight when it comes to setting your fees. So will the amount you choose to (or have to) pay yourself. In addition, of course, you'll need to deal with the question of exactly how much it's "realistic" to ask a client to pay for your work; in other words, what your market value is. In this chapter, we'll be looking at both factors, and I'll pass along some suggestions on how you can best use each of these indicators to determine your fee structure.

Billing: The Options

Typically, a consultant will charge by the day. It's not uncommon, however, for certain consultants to charge by the hour or on a project basis. If you've established an exceptionally strong relationship with a firm, you can charge by the year! Still other consultants will ask for a retainer, and then, after working enough hours to exhaust the money already paid, bill for the balance.

So there are a variety of billing options open to you. Most beginning consultants start out charging by the day; this allows them a certain amount of flexibility, and doesn't require clients to commit to large retainer fees or salary-like arrangements. Keep in mind that I said "salary-*like*." Because you don't work for your client as an employee, there are a lot of advantages to salaried employment that you'll probably forego as a consultant. Company-subsidized health and vacation benefits usually head this list.

The Battle of the Budget

Obviously, there has to be some correlation between what you charge and what you spend in order to stay alive and keep working as a consultant. If you find, for example, that it costs you one hundred dollars a day to maintain yourself, and you charge fifty dollars a day, you will eventually notice a discrepancy somewhere—even if you work every day! (And working with clients every day, as we've seen, isn't really an option.)

Now, the example I just used may seem overly broad, but that very problem can creep up on you over time, especially at the beginning stages of your practice. Virtually every business must incorporate a process called *capitalization*. (That's "arranging seed money" to you and me.)

Determining what is—and isn't—profitable activity is often a difficult endeavor, and it can require particularly close attention at the outset of your work as a consultant, when your initial capitalization plans may allow you to overextend yourself without even knowing it.

Most people capitalize their businesses by going to a bank and asking for a loan. I'm going to assume here that you will attempt to follow that route, though I should say that it's highly unlikely that you'll be able to get a loan without putting up your own personal property as collateral. While banks are familiar with loaning to, say, manufacturing ventures, they see virtually nothing they can repossess in a beginning consulting business. Consequently, most loan officers will take a dim view of approving an application that carries with it what they view as an unjustifiable risk.

Let's begin at the beginning. How do you determine the minimum level you should charge your clients—the "floor," if you will? You draw up a budget.

What You Need, What You Plan to Pay for It, and How Much It All Adds Up To

Here is a standard monthly budget that a beginning consultant might come up with before determining the level of capitalization he or she will require. It's not *the* standard budget, but one possible version. There are, of course, as many different budgets as there are companies to break them.

Note the comparatively low amount of money spent on marketing and advertising. This luxury is possible only because of a decision to pursue the remarkably cost-effective option of cold calling, as we discussed in an earlier chapter. A business plan that takes a pass on cold calling will have to incorporate a great many more marketing dollars in its budget.

Monthly Budget

Accounting	100.00
Bank Loan Payments	200.00
Dues and Subscriptions	15.00
Equipment	50.00
Insurance	50.00
Legal and Accounting	250.00
Messenger/Air Express	75.00
Office Supplies	50.00
Postage	100.00
Printed Items (Promotional)	100.00
Rent	2,000.00
Salaries	????
Telephone/Long Distance	300.00

A Room, a Telephone, and a Desk . . .

If you're astute, you'll notice that I left blank a very important line on that budget. We'll talk about salaries in a second.

As it turns out, the total on the prototype monthly budget I've used above comes to $3,290.00—less salaries. That's the amount that will give you a telephone number to pass out to people, a batch of business cards, a room to sit in, and maybe a desk.

You haven't satisfied a single customer yet. You haven't arranged even one assignment. And odds are that you've done nothing to establish yourself as an expert in your field. But there you are, paying nearly $3,500 a month for the privilege of saying, "I'm a consultant; here's my phone number; this is my office address."

Do You Need to Eat?

When it comes to setting your own salary, you have to look at a lot of factors. Are you dependent on the revenue of the business for tomorrow afternoon's trip to the supermarket? Do you live in New York City or Omaha, Nebraska? What kind of lifestyle are you supporting?

If you're like most of us, you don't have an unlimited amount of money in your savings account. The option of taking a pass on any salary for the first few years probably isn't realistic—no matter how much sense it might make to your accountant.

You should realize, however, that your first year or so of work probably isn't the time to establish extravagant standards as far as your personal income from the business is concerned. The best course is to select a salary that allows you to make ends meet while you establish yourself. I'm not suggesting that you starve yourself, merely that you recognize that even a modest salary—as we'll learn shortly—translates into a pretty impressive daily rate.

Let's say for the sake of argument you decide to pay yourself the very modest sum of $24,000 a year, or $2,000 a month. That means your total budgeted monthly expenses come out to . . .

$5,290.00

Now it's time for an important question. How many days a month are you going to work?

Don't even think about saying thirty. Consulting is an intensely customer-oriented business, and customers are in their offices, as a general rule, from nine in the morning till five at night, Monday through Friday. You can't prospect from nine in the evening until midnight on Saturday, no matter how hard you try, because no one is going to pick up the telephone.

You can't meet with your clients at six in the morning because they won't show up. Besides which, you will probably go insane if you work too many thirty-day months.

Say twenty. But wait! You're not going to be seeing clients for all twenty of those days, are you? You're going to be prospecting for, say, ten of them! So the actual *billable* days you have at your disposal to meet your overhead and salary costs is reduced to ten.

$$5,290.00/10 \text{ days} = 529.00$$

There you have it. Roughly five hundred and thirty dollars a day under your present budget. That's the *minimum* you're asking your client to pay for your services. That's the floor.

But before you go print up the rate sheets and flyers, take another look at the numbers. Some of the costs we've examined are more or less set in stone. You have to have a telephone. It should be clear, though, that there are some variables that are still under your control. Take the whole issue of office space, for example. Leaving aside the possibilities of the tax breaks involved (which I trust you'll review with an accountant), if you can work out of your home instead of renting an office, you'll cut over a third from your operating budget!

It's possible that your insurance or bank costs could vary significantly from what I've set up here. Remember that it's not *my* budget that matters, but *yours*.

Once you see what you have to do, you'll know what you're really working toward. In the example we just looked at, we know that you have to take in $5,290 every month. Now if you've somehow gotten a loan from the bank (or from a supportive relative), and the first six months or so that you're operating, you take in an average of only two thousand dollars a month, something is seriously wrong. *Even if you've got money left in the bank from your loan,* something is wrong and needs to be examined fast. You're missing your target by a mile—even if you are charging your clients the "right" amount.

The Upper Limits

So much for the floor. How about the ceiling?

As a provider of business services, you will have to be the judge of the market forces at work in your consulting practice. I can't do that for you because I don't know your competition, I don't know what your background is, and I don't know what kind of feedback your first clients can be expected to give you.

My general advice to those starting out in consulting, however, is to charge the amount that it takes you to deliver a superior job—and provides what you consider to be a comfortable living—for the first year or so.

It's possible, of course, that I'm being overcautious. It's possible that people are going to fall all over you and engage in intense bidding wars for your work, right from the start. If that happens, you have my congratulations. You're obviously doing something right, and if you want to raise your rates, that's your call. But most people getting into this business really don't have the credentials or the reputation to demand top dollar from the moment they step into someone's office the first time.

And by the way, if you do charge unrealistically high rates early on, and then land an assignment, woe unto you if the job falls apart and you can't deliver what you outlined in your proposal. Reputations tend to plummet rapidly when large dollar amounts get poured down the drain at no apparent advantage to the client.

You can't charge people for a reputation that doesn't yet exist. Let your focus in the early months be on delivering superior service at realistic rates. If you do, you'll probably find the prestige assignments with top-level fees waiting for you a few years down the line.

CHAPTER 6

Sample Proposals and Related Documents

The Real Thing

The proposals, letters, and schedules I've included in this chapter aren't hypothetical documents with no base in reality. They're based on *actual correspondence* I conducted with a number of my own accounts. (Names and some other pertinent details have been altered.)

In this part of the book, we'll examine the various stages an assignment will pass through, from the initial written contact to the evaluation of the project.

Use these examples as a model, but remember that every business is different; your services and client requirements will require that you tailor your approach carefully to each account.

Before the Sale

The first correspondence with a prospect you've contacted by phone should probably be brief and to the point. No further material need be included than a simple restatement of the agreement to meet on a given date, and a word of thanks to the prospect for taking the time to talk with you in the first place.

You can, of course, compose letters to prospects who *haven't* scheduled appointments with you. Usually these take the form of a congratulatory note on a promotion or similar accomplishment, or a brief explanation about a book or article you're enclosing. Don't pressure the prospect, but don't be afraid to tactfully remind him or her of your practice and its services. These letters, too, should be short and to the point.

All of these letters can play an important part in laying the groundwork for a successful future business relationship. Here are two samples you can use as models.

Preproposal *"Thank You"* Letter

Mr. Nicholas Bennett
First Vice President
Greenville Electric
50 Main Street
Anytown, USA 00000

Dear Nick:

I'm pleased we had the opportunity to discuss by phone the ways in which D.E.I. Management Group has helped other firms reach their sales goals.

I look forward to seeing you next week to continue our discussion.

Best personal regards.

Sincerely,

Stephan Schiffman

Stephan Schiffman
President, D.E.I. Management Group

Congratulatory "Keep in Touch" Letter

Mr. Nathan Stanley
Regional Vice President
Melville Machinery
75 Blue Ridge Drive
Anytown, USA 00000

Dear Nathan:

I was happy to read in the latest issue of Gear and Sprocket *that you'd finally gotten the recognition you had coming after all those years at the Dwightville facility. Congratulations on the leap to the executive lounge!*

The magazine also mentioned that you'd be retaining your sizable influence over the sales staff there at Melville. As I mentioned in our last conversation, I have a lot of ideas we should take the time to review. Perhaps after you've settled into the new office we can talk.

We should get together soon. I'm working on some very successful programs with other firms in your field.

Again, congratulations on the promotion. Let's keep in touch.

Sincerely,

Stephan Schiffman

Stephan Schiffman
President, D.E.I. Management Group

Cover Letter and Proposal (#1)

Following is a sample proposal for an educational institution interested in streamlining its development efforts and conducting more successful fundraising campaigns.

Proposal

for

Volunteer Development Program

Southeastern State University

D.E.I. Management Group, Inc.

888 Seventh Avenue

New York, NY 10106

Mr. Mark Iverson
Southeastern State University
25 West Rye Street
Anytown, USA 00000

Dear Mark:

I am pleased that we had the opportunity to meet and discuss the ways in which D.E.I. Management Group could be of service to Southeastern State. This proposal will outline a four-step program that will assist you in:

1. Gaining the support of your membership.
2. Giving specific instruction and assistance in fundraising techniques.
3. Increasing the overall visibility of your development office.

We look forward to working with you on what we know will be an exciting and rewarding project.

Sincerely,

Stephan Schiffman

Stephan Schiffman
President
D.E.I. Management Group, Inc.

Introduction

Since 1979, D.E.I. Management Group has developed and constructed training programs for corporations and nonprofit organizations throughout the United States. Some of our clients have included American Communication, T&T Data, and Honeyline Equipment. We've also worked with a host of smaller, nonprofit organizations, including Waltham State University.

We are experts at providing in-house training that shows your people exactly how to meet or exceed their income goals. We take a pragmatic approach to our work that includes rigorous follow-through leads to measurable success for our clients.

We strive to work with you in order to develop a program that will institute realistic goals and yield positive results in a reasonable period of time.

The program outlined in this proposal for the Office of University Development and Alumni Relations will offer the following benefits:

1. *The first program will act as a kickoff opportunity for a series of four additional meetings to be conducted over the coming year. The ongoing character of the work will keep the topics fresh and relevant over a period of months, not days.*
2. *The series will not only be geared to fundraising topics, but also incorporate personal development issues, thereby broadening interest on the part of the Southeast State staff.*

3. *D.E.I. Management Group will act as seminar coordinator for the programs.*

D.E.I. Management Group suggests the following schedule of programs.

Kickoff Program: Proposed date 5-3-01

This will incorporate three elements: a breakfast meeting, seminars, and a closing luncheon. Two parallel sessions will be held; this feature enables participants to attend both of the day's seminars. These seminars will cover the following topics:

Seminar A: Motivating Yourself and Others
This portion of the program will be conducted by Stephan Schiffman, the President of D.E.I. Management Group. Mr. Schiffman will focus on ways in which individuals can learn to motivate themselves and others in order to attain personal and business goals.

Seminar B: Leadership Skills in Today's Business World
A panel discussion, with alumni members participating, on today's business problems.

D.E.I. Management Group will conduct three additional programs on leadership skills during the course of this year. These include the following:

Effective Face-to-Face Solicitation for the New Volunteer: Proposed date 9-10-01

This is a highly successful ninety-minute presentation covering face-to-face skills volunteers can use in soliciting for the alumni association.

Telephone Solicitation Skills for the Volunteer and Staff: Proposed date 11-12-01

Topics covered include: how to become more effective on the phone, gaining new contributors, and the art of winning renewal on previous donations.

Personal Motivation for Today's Businessperson: Proposed date 1-14-02

Staffers learn how to establish goals and attain their personal objectives.

Other services include talks on the following issues:

1. *Time management*
2. *Dealing with stress*
3. *Leadership skills and team building*

Follow-Through Program: Proposed date 2-12-02

Staffers evaluate their progress toward income goals and receive one-on-one counseling to assure implementation of key principles.

Dates on these events are flexible. These programs would commence with a buffet dinner at approximately 6:00 P.M.

About D.E.I. Management Group

Stephan Schiffman *is a Certified Management Consultant. He conducts approximately three hundred seminars yearly on a nationwide basis. His background features work in a variety of communications, broadcasting, psychotherapy, and brokerage services. Mr. Schiffman, who is listed in* Who's Who In Finance and Industry, *is a member of the National Speakers Association, International Management Consultants, and the Society of Professional Management Consultants. He is a frequent guest on talk shows and is a successful author. His book* Cold Calling Techniques (That Really Work!) *recently entered its fourth edition.*

Walter Currier, *who serves as D.E.I. Management Group's National Sales Manager, has held that position for approximately two years. Prior to that, Mr. Currier was Midwest Region Sales Manager for a major pharmaceutical firm.*

Larraine Randall, *a Senior Consultant for D.E.I. Management Group, worked in private practice as an attorney for ten years before deciding to enter the field of organizational development. Ms. Randall is presently a candidate for her Ph.D. at Morris University, and has extensive experience in conducting organizational development programs with major U.S. corporations.*

Fee Structure

D.E.I. Management will act as seminar coordinator for this series, including the three additional buffet meetings, for $5,550.

Fee Schedule

50%   Upon agreement
10%   After first program
10%   After second program
10%   After third program
20%   Upon completion of all programs

Cover Letter and Proposal (#2)

Here is an advanced sales training program for a medium-size banking institution.

Throughout the proposal, techniques are described in enough detail to pique the reader's interest, but retain specifics to be covered in the program itself.

Proposal

for

Sales Training Program

Lonborg National Bank

D.E.I. Management Group, Inc.

888 Seventh Avenue

New York, NY 10106

Mr. Michael Levin
Lonborg National Bank
Metro Plaza
P.O. Box 1967
Anytown USA 00000

Dear Michael:

D.E.I. Management Group is pleased to present this proposal for the implementation of a 2–day sales training program for new representatives at the Lonborg Bank.

As I mentioned in our phone conversation, I intend to make use of videotape in the role-playing portions of the program.

The program is designed as a workshop and practicum and offers specific skills that will:

- *increase sales awareness*
- *teach sales skills*
- *integrate sales into the bank culture*

I look forward to working with you on what I know will be a rewarding and exciting project.

Sincerely,

Stephan Schiffman

Stephan Schiffman
President, D.E.I. Management Group

Since 1979, D.E.I. Management Group has developed sales and motivational training programs for Fortune 500 companies, as well as smaller organizations. Our clients have included ABC Communications, Tykkon Oil and Energy, Compulectronics International, Bank USA, and National Easthampton Bank. As a result of our banking experience, we are able to offer programs that will meet the needs of new commercial lenders at Lonborg.

The proposal is specifically targeted toward the new commercial lender who, after completing the product training program at Lonborg, now needs to develop specific selling skills in order to be effective in a competitive marketplace.

The program itself is a two-day lecture and practicum that offers the opportunity not only to learn the skills, but also to hone and develop them to full effectiveness.

Methodology

Since D.E.I. Management Group has worked with many banks in developing a variety of sales programs, the firm understands the potential scope of Lonborg's needs. Initially, D.E.I. Management Group will meet with you and key members of your staff in order to establish the specific requirements of the sales group. D.E.I. Management Group will then conduct a 2–day program for all new sales personnel. Selling skills are taught on a step-by-step basis, and incorporate the following topics:

- *Theory of sales and sales cycle*
- *Basic product training*

- *Introduction to selling skills*
- *Prospecting and appointment making*
- *Listening and negotiation skills*
- *Handling objections and turnaround*
- *Closing skills*
- *Reinforcement*
- *Sales management*

While the assumption is that each participant has already been exposed to sufficient product training, D.E.I. Management Group will work with senior staff to identify problem areas and focus on ongoing product education. In addition, D.E.I. will offer the option to renew the program to ensure correct training for future Lonborg sales personnel.

Program Outline

The program itself will adhere to the following outline:

1. *Prospecting and cross selling*
2. *Presentation skills*
3. *Listening and negotiation skills*
4. *Closing skills*
5. *Understanding the selling cycle*
6. *Personal goal orientation*
7. *Follow-through program*

Where appropriate, videotape will be used in all role-playing and practice sessions.

1. Prospecting and cross selling

During this session, participants will learn ways in which they can develop additional leads. Since selling is based upon contacting individuals, it is necessary to hone these skills in order to be more effective. During this session individuals make cold calls and use specific techniques in face-to-face encounters with prospects as well. The entire referral process is discussed, with particular emphasis placed on the topics of developing relationships with existing customers and generating new contacts. The "By the Way" technique is employed as a method of increasing consumer response to and interest in a variety of Lonborg services.

2. Presentation skills

It is necessary in selling to make an effective presentation. During this stage of the program, participants learn how to interview the prospective buyer properly—in order to determine specific needs. Product knowledge now comes into play. (It is a necessary prerequisite of the program that individuals have some degree of product awareness and knowledge.)

3. Listening and negotiation skills

D.E.I. Management Group stresses, through an interactive teaching approach, ways in which individuals can improve their listening skills and negotiation skills. Since both the buyer and the seller want to win, it is important that a win-win situation be the end result—and, of course, the initial goal—of a sales call. This is outlined and discussed in detail. At the same time, the participants have the opportunity to "test out" their new-found knowledge in practical exchanges, discussions, and role-playing during this session. Participants learn that listening and negotiation skills become increasingly important in higher levels of sales, but are the basis for all sales on any level.

4. Closing skills

There are seven different ways in which a sales person can close a sale. The most practical of the group is addressed first in this section: the close in which an assumption is made that a prospect will become a buyer. Discussion typically leads to a variety of other situations and scenarios, which are fully discussed and played out. Emphasis is placed on the ways in which the participant can turn around the objections that inevitably follow the suggestion of a purchase. In addition, participants learn to help the individual develop a closer relationship with Lonborg. It is not necessary to engage in a "hard sell" at this point, but it is necessary to be persistent in order to achieve the goal. The distinction between a "hard sell" and a "persistent sell" is examined. This is a crucial point, as too much persistence without having laid the proper groundwork will destroy the sale. Bankers, after all, have a unique opportunity to develop relationships with their existing customer base. Therefore, customer relationships and their development are emphasized in the closing skills section, and fit comfortably in that cycle.

5. Selling cycle

In this section, participants learn how to predict their closing rate, how to determine their optimum number of prospects, and how to rank the prospects according to the category of success achieved within a given group. Participants understand the selling cycle and at the same time learn how to fill the "pipeline" on an ongoing basis—in other words, maintaining a constant pool of qualified leads—by using prospecting and cross selling skills.

6. Personal goal orientation

It is necessary for an individual who is selling to understand how that sale directly affects his or her income and goals. Too often we find that salespeople have inadequate goal preparation, and the motivation achieved in a goal-orientation process is important and emphasized at this juncture.

7. Follow-through program

We propose a half-day follow-through program on February 19, 2002. Participants will evaluate their progress toward income goals and receive one-on-one counseling to assure implementation of key principles.

Tentative Outline of Program

Day 1 (A.M.)

- *Theory of Selling*
- *Prospecting and Cross Selling (P.M.)*
- *Presentation Skills*

Day 2 (A.M.)

- *Listening and Negotiation Skills (P.M.)*
- *Closing Skills*

Day 3 (A.M.)

- *Personal Goal Orientation*

Follow-through Program (Half-day)

- *Monitoring Progress Over Time*

Projected Dates

- *February 29th, 1999*
- *March 1st and 2nd, 1999*

Fee Structure

Anticipated number of participants will be twenty. Per person cost will be $625 plus materials: approximately $20 per person including all workbooks and text.

Total estimated cost: $12,900

Payment Schedule

25%	*Upon agreement*
50%	*Before the program*
25% plus expenses	*10 days after completion*

They Said "Yes"!

Once a client agrees to work with you, you should follow up immediately with a "thank you" note.

In addition, you'll need to provide the contact with a letter of agreement. Each communication constitutes an important part of your work with the client; promptness, neatness, and accuracy on your part will be noticed.

Post-Sale (but Preassignment) "Thank You" Letter

Mr. Bruce C. Lancaster
Executive Vice President
Carlton Manufacturing
20 Green Street
Anytown USA 00000

Thank you for allowing D.E.I. Management Group to be of service to Carlton.

We look forward to working with you on what we know will be an exciting and rewarding project.

Sincerely,

Stephan Schiffman

Stephan Schiffman
President

Letter of Agreement

Note: Your consulting practice is unique. Use the letter below as a point of reference, but consult with your attorney before drafting or signing any contract or letter of agreement.

Mr. Joseph Mallory
Vice President/Director of Training
Edison Regional Savings Bank
600 Parrish Road
Anytown USA 00000

Dear Joe:

Please let this serve as a letter of agreement between Edison Regional Savings Bank and D.E.I. Management Group for conducting a Cold-Calling Outreach Program for the bank.

As per our proposal and subsequent conversation, it is agreed that D.E.I. Management Group will conduct no less than six (6) programs on the following dates:

- October 16
- October 29
- November 16
- November 17
- November 18
- November 19

Each program will be for a full day, and includes lecture, group participation, and role-playing. We anticipate that approximately twenty people will be present

---

at each session. For purposes of this agreement, the total fee for the program will be $13,500, as outlined in our proposal. Our travel costs will be billed as $100, and there will be no additional mileage costs unless there is a change in locale on the part of Edison Regional Savings Bank. It is also agreed that if a program is canceled by Edison Regional Savings Bank, and subsequent rescheduling is not made within a reasonable period of time, Edison Regional Savings Bank will pay the prorated fee for that date.

The fee payment schedule is as follows:

25%   Upon agreement
30%   November 1, 1999
45%   Plus expenses, December 1, 1999

You will be invoiced.

We look forward to working with you on what we know is going to be an exciting and rewarding project.

Best personal regards.

Sincerely,

Stephan Schiffman

Stephan Schiffman
President, D.E.I. Management Group

After the Dust Settles . . .

Even when the assignment is complete, quite a bit of work remains to be done.

Of course, a "thank you" letter is in order. In addition, you should provide your client with a detailed evaluation of the work you've done. (This evaluation provides you with a very real opportunity to make arrangements for additional work.)

And, of course, you must bill the client for the amount due. A sample invoice is enclosed.

Postassignment "Thank You" Letter

Mr. Brian Richards
Senior Sales Manager
Glimmer Light Fixtures
1000 North Twin Towers Plaza
Anytown USA 00000

Dear Brian:

I just wanted to drop a note to tell you how happy I was
with the program we wrapped up yesterday.

Your staff is enthusiastic, hardworking, and eager to
put new techniques into action. I have no doubt that
you'll start to see positive results in short order.

My formal evaluation will follow shortly.

Sincerely,

Stephan Schiffman

Stephan Schiffman
President, D.E.I. Management Group

Evaluation

Mr. David Cross
Executive Vice President
CNS Marine
20 Towson Street
Anytown USA

Dear David:

The following will serve as a brief report on the progress of the CNS Sales Training Program. Specific recommendations are also listed.

Training

D.E.I. Management Group conducted four (4) half-day sessions for CNS sales representatives. Material covered included telephone cold-calling techniques which involved the development of a script, tracking of calls, and methodology of handling and turning around objections. The second session focused on the results of the telephone calls, as well as on proper ways to open and close a sale. The sales staff now has the tools necessary to increase sales activity.

We will follow up these two sessions with a half-day program to be conducted in November. At that time we will reiterate some of the key points and review telephone and sales work.

Calling Results

We tracked calls that were made by the participants and found that the following totals were logged by CNS personnel:

720 dials
465 completed calls
78 appointments

The resulting contacts-to-appointments ratio comes to 17 to 1.

As you know from the points covered both in the program and in my proposal, total sales are dependent upon prospecting efforts. In order for CNS to register a substantial increase in sales, the total number of calls and appointments must be increased.

We will work with CNS over the following weeks to implement a tracking system that will allow you to evaluate the prospecting activities of each salesperson.

Recommendations

1. *D.E.I. Management Group will conduct a followup program over the coming weeks, as described above. Even with such efforts, however, CNS must monitor on-site sales efforts continuously. We suggest that you give serious thought to installing a regional manager who can "float" from branch to branch, working with each representative on a daily basis.*

2. The monthly meeting discussing sales activities should be maintained.

3. We would give great credence to the development of a telemarketing unit that would work out of the Anytown office.

Invoice

October 3, 1999
The Megalith Savings Bank
678 Main St.
Anytown, NJ 00000

Attn: Mr. Nicholas H. Jardiniere

INVOICE

Fee for program	$6,400.00
Sept. 30 —	$1,500
Sept. 28 —	1,500
Sept. 23 —	1,500
Sept. 21 —	1,500
Follow-up fee —	400*
16 Manuals @ $11.25 ea.	180.00
	$6,580.00
Due upon receipt	$6,180.00

*Follow-up fee ($400) due upon completion of assignment.

TO:
D.E.I. Management Group, Inc.
850 Seventh Ave.
New York, NY 10019

mtd/1500

CHAPTER 7

How Will You Keep Track of It All?

Growth—and Its Consequences

In this chapter, we'll be examining many of the problems your consulting practice will experience as a result of growth.

Obviously, you want your business to grow. If you don't want it to grow, I'd strongly suggest you take another look at your business plan. Anticipating no growth whatsoever simply doesn't make sense for most practices. If you honestly want yours to stay small and/or service only the same few clients over and over again, there's a very good likelihood that your practice will stagnate and eventually die.

So if we assume that growth is part of the plan, we have to acknowledge—*ahead of time*—that the growth is going to carry with it some implications. We examined this problem a little earlier in the book, when we took a broad overview of the "typical" first few years of a consulting practice.

In time, of course, you may expand to the point that you take on "associates"—new, bright people who are as well versed in problem solving in your area as you are. But even that rosy prospect, having so much business that you can't handle it all and must locate new personnel, carries potential difficulties. How will you feel about doing business with clients who may never meet you face-to-face? How certain can you be of the quality of work turned in by the associate? Will your work philosophies differ radically?

In many areas of your business, you will find that growth can be a two-edged sword, often offering as many complications as opportunities. Now it's time to address the issue of growth in a little more detail. I'm going to offer some adjustments—not solutions, mind you, but adjustments—that I think you should try to incorporate *from the very beginning*, so that you aren't taken by surprise when the problems that accompany rapid growth start to surface.

Collections: You Come First

You should, by this point, be familiar with the target figure you established earlier when you composed your monthly budget—the number of dollars you must take in every month in order to continue your business.

There are many, many things that can get in the way of your making that amount. Nothing in that category is quite as frustrating, however, as performing work for which you aren't paid. Being paid late runs a close second.

We learned a few chapters back why simply presenting an invoice at the completion of the project isn't the best idea in the world. You don't want to sit around waiting for bills to come in for months on end.

The sad fact is, however, that on a certain percentage of your accounts, you're going to. You can try to buck this trend, but you can't completely eliminate it. Every business has to deal with bad debt, and there's no reason your consulting practice should be any different. Large companies deal with this problem by creating complicated billing and collections departments, or by hiring outside companies. You're not a large company . . . yet.

Your practice is, at this stage, a small company. And as it grows, its percentage of bad debt is going to grow, too. If the question of uncollectable invoices seems intangible or insignificant to you now—if you feel confident that you can keep an eye on all the overdue accounts without too much trouble, take a brief moment and do yourself a big favor. Imagine your business twice as large as it is now. Perhaps three times or even ten times as large. That's what you're shooting for, right? As soon as that growth takes place, your overdue file is going to get two, three, or ten times as large, as well, and there's a decent chance that its growth may even outstrip your company's. Bad debt will get your attention sooner or later, I guarantee it.

So what do you do? You start to take pre-emptive measures *now* to minimize the problem.

Once you're big enough to have an accounts receivable and/or collections department you may have less to worry about. But for the present you should concentrate on making the time you have now, *before* the accounts become overdue, work to your advantage. That way you'll spend less time tracking people down and asking for money in the future. (You should be keenly aware, by now, of the importance of keeping to your own personal schedule. Obviously, blowing half a day every week tracking down your money isn't going to do much for your productivity.)

Tips for Keeping Your Receivables from Going Unreceived

Request 25 percent of your total estimated fee before you do any work, as specified earlier in this book. For some jobs it may be appropriate to seek more than this figure; for others it may be appropriate to ask for less. Try in every case to receive some payment before beginning the assignment. It may be advisable to accept a slightly lower fee in order to be sure of receiving money in advance. If you don't receive 25 percent or something very close to it, don't begin the project. (If you feel you must make an exception to this practice, be absolutely positive that your first payment is being processed, and ask for the specific date you can expect the first check.)

Invoice your accounts immediately. Here's the sequence you should follow.

- Presentation
- Client Accepts Proposal
- Handshake
- You Go Home, Write, and Send a Thank You Letter
- You Wait Two Days (Unless Schedule Dictates Otherwise)
- You Send Letter of Agreement
- Letter of Agreement Is Signed
- You Receive Letter of Agreement
- You Send Invoice for First Payment

Make sure that the company receives your invoices on the dates you specify in your proposal. Bill larger companies as early in the month as possible.

Arrange special payment plans with firms that have large accounting departments (and thus tend to pay slowly). Try to submit one or two bills very early on in the process. The largest corporations—and most governmental bodies—hold onto their bills for a very long time indeed. Be prepared for this.

Be certain that the smaller companies you work with are solvent. Large firms, as a general rule, may take their time, but will attend to their debts. Small businesses can sometimes be extremely cavalier about "details" like satisfying their creditors. In your meetings with other consultants, you will probably come across quite a few who simply won't work with small firms.

Keep written records of all your agreements with clients. If you must ever institute any legal proceeding against a customer who will not pay you for work you've done, it's important to be able to provide appropriate documentation.

Tips for Collecting Overdue Accounts

Be fanatical about sending invoices over the course of the project. The day a payment is missed, send a duplicate invoice and a tactful reminder. (A sample invoice can be found elsewhere in this book.) Continue to send reminders every ten days. Once the bill has reached a certain age (for many accounts, this might be thirty days), proceed to the next step and . . .

Make a polite phone call reminding your client of the payment terms specified in your contract. This will usually do the trick. If it doesn't . . .

Evaluate the account. Don't needlessly antagonize contacts you've worked hard to establish, but don't let a smaller firm off the hook if it has no real intention to pay your bill. Where appropriate, send a concise letter to a department head outlining your problem, and expressing confidence that the problem can be resolved to everyone's satisfaction.

Obviously, it's preferable to make certain that your terms are understood and agreed to from the moment you begin work on a project. But on those accounts that somehow miss the mark, make every effort to pursue the debt as promptly and effectively as possible.

The End of the Project: Upsides and Downsides

As your practice gets larger, you may begin to feel swamped by work. It's possible that you'll have a number of different projects going at once. In these situations, time management takes on even more importance. You'll save yourself a lot of time and aggravation if you realize—and, eventually, learn to anticipate—the positive and negative implications presented by a job that's nearing its conclusion.

A project's completion can be a time of unparalleled opportunity. It can also represent a setback for your practice.

Let's look first at the opportunities. You complete the assignment. Everyone's thrilled with your work. Your evaluation of the work you've done, as well as the new direction taken by the department you've been cooperating with, is absolutely flawless. Everything's worked out marvelously. Why shouldn't you continue with a similar challenge elsewhere in the company—or perhaps even keep your efforts focused along the lines you've been working, to achieve even more remarkable results?

It's a nice ending. And it can happen. The most important factor influencing such a conclusion, of course, is that of the quality of your work. It has to be superior. Beyond that, there are some "nudges" you can incorporate that will help you to move toward this model conclusion on more and more of your assignments.

First of all, you can structure your letter of agreement and proposal so that *renewal is virtually automatic.* This is a technique that must, of course, be discussed openly with your contact—doing otherwise will make you look a little shaky as far as ethics are concerned. Such an arrangement is not uncommon among larger firms. It's rare that a middle-size or small company will opt for this arrangement, but it might not hurt to try. Your proposal might feature an "option to renew at completion."

That option, of course, would represent your chance to convince your contact of the benefits of "continuing along the same lines we've set up." Such ongoing business can do quite a lot for your practice.

Secondly, you can bear in mind that being a consultant really means that you are *constantly in a job search mode*. Simply put, the fact that you're working on an assignment doesn't mean that your prospecting instincts must lie dormant. As you work on a given project, you can keep an eye out for new projects that might benefit the organization you're working for, and perhaps even "overlap" assignments—prepare a proposal for one while you're working on another. Obviously, you wouldn't charge the firm that's engaged you for the privilege of having you write a proposal!

That's the opportunity section of the story. Now for the crisis segment.

Assignments can—and often do—end abruptly. Clients can change their minds. It's possible that your contact may have second thoughts about your consulting services for any number of reasons, including: unforeseen budgetary pressures; internal political problems; pressing new departmental or company goals, requiring overtime from the people with whom you're working; or even dissatisfaction with your work.

Whatever the reason, your reaction *must remain professional*. The fact that the assignment is over doesn't mean that your relationship with the client is over. Try to get the best possible information about what went wrong, and then do your best not to burn any bridges. *Always remember that you aren't an employee.* The client has, in ninety-nine cases out of a hundred, made no long-term commitment to you. The fact that no long-term commitment exists is one of the most attractive things about hiring a consultant.

Of course, if you've completed a substantial amount of the work, and are told that the assignment, along with the payment due to you, has been canceled, you're not in a great position.

You can, in that situation, do two things subsequent to your exhaustive efforts to collect from the firm. First, you can talk to an attorney about the amount of money you have a legal right to claim from the company for services rendered. Your attorney will want to see copies of your letter of agreement and proposal. Second, you can consider that you've learned a valuable lesson in the importance of establishing *ongoing payment plans*—plans that allow you to collect 75 percent of your money once you've completed 75 percent of the work. Such plans, as we've discussed already, offer you much-needed protection from the whims of both accounting departments and disagreeable management decisions.

"Who Authorized This? Oh, Right. Me."

Right now, it's probably not a big deal for you to run down to the corner drugstore, buy a bunch of supplies, and keep the receipts for tax purposes. You need ballpoint pens. You're out of ballpoint pens. So you go buy some.

It will not always be so cut-and-dried. The day will come when your carefully established budgets for office supplies, equipment, outside clerical or accounting help, and postage will be in constant danger of being shattered by overspending, unauthorized charges, and duplication. These problems tend to grow in alarming, exponential fashion, and the day will probably come when you open up your desk drawer, find no stationery, order a new shipment on an (expensive!) rush basis, then, two days later, find that a fresh, unopened stack of virgin reams has been waiting in your basement to be discovered.

Try to forecast your requirements for supplies and services on a monthly basis. Monitor your inventories of essential items. Wherever possible, write purchase orders whenever you need to buy something—even if you're the only person who sees them. You'll be able to identify, verify, and categorize every business purchase you make, and that's as it should be.

(Note: You'll find a sample purchase order as well as some other useful business forms at the end of this book. Use them as a model for the ones you'll use in your own practice.)

CHAPTER 8

How Much Money Will You Need?

Cash Flow

How much "seed money" will you need in order to survive through your first year in business?

As you might imagine, the answer is a complicated one. But let's take a stab at it and look at the whole issue of cash flow in a way that will show you how you can begin to address the issue in your own business.

The best way to begin is probably to work in very round— maybe *unrealistically* round—figures. That will keep things clear, and it will also serve as a reminder that the figures bear no relationship to *your* consulting practice. Your financial needs and levels of income are, of course, unique. The final picture you arrive at should probably be reviewed with your banker or financial advisor, and it wouldn't hurt to go over things with your accountant, either.

The First Crucial Months

Let's say that your consulting business has monthly expenditures of exactly $1,000. And let's say that one sale constitutes $500 worth of income for your practice.

January

It's January, and you've just begun your practice. We know that, over the course of January, you're going to spend $1,000. How much income are you going to take in?

More than likely, zero dollars. The first month, you'll be doing a lot of things—marketing, strategizing, meeting people—actually *collecting* on jobs probably isn't going to happen right off the bat. So what's your position at the end of January?

It's negative numbers time, to the tune of $1,000. Merely by existing you've spent that much, and you haven't taken anything in. The chart you see here—a simplified version of the cash-flow sheet you'll find at the end of this book—illustrates the point:

Month of: January
Sales Made: Zero
Dollars Collected: Zero

	Jan	Feb	Mar	Apr	May	Jun
Inflow						
Cash on hand beginning of month:	0					
Inflow:	—					
Outflow						
Cash outflow (see monthly budget):	1,000					
Net cash on hand, end of month:	−1,000					

February

February now. How much are you going to spend? Again, the answer is easy. Every month equals $1,000 in expenditures. How much do you take in? Well, let's say you make a sale this month—chalk it up to all that hard work in January. But . . . how much of the money will you actually see *in February?*

I've emphasized in previous chapters how important it is to try to collect your fees promptly, even to the point of collecting a portion of your fee before beginning any work whatsoever. Here's where the importance of that advice will really come home to you. Let's play conservatively—after all, we're trying to determine how *much* capitalization you'll need, not how little—and say that you decide *not* to require any payment from your first account before you begin work.

Let's be even more cruel and say that you're "lucky" enough to make your first sale to a Fortune 500 corporation. Prestigious, right? Keep telling yourself that. You'll need all the prestige you can get. Especially considering that you'll be waiting ninety days to receive your first dollar as a consultant.

So much for February: No revenue this month either, and you won't receive payment for that first job until sometime in late May.

After approximately sixty days in business, here's the scoreboard:

Month of: February
Sales Made: One
Dollars Collected: Zero

	Jan	Feb	Mar	Apr	May	Jun
Inflow						
Cash on hand beginning of month:	0	−1,000				
Inflow:	—	—				
Outflow						
Cash outflow (see monthly budget):	1,000	1,000				
Net cash on hand, end of month:	-1,000	-2,000				

March

March. Things pick up. You finally make a splash, landing three sales—more than enough to reach the $1,000 target level that will, at least theoretically, even out your expenditures. But there's no revenue yet. You're still working with "prestigious" (and slow-paying) firms. Your references are beginning to look great. Your bank account, however, is another story.

Month of: March
Sales Made: Three
Dollars Collected: Zero

	Jan	Feb	Mar	Apr	May	Jun
Inflow						
Cash on hand beginning of month:	0	−1,000	−2,000			
Inflow:	—	—	—			
Outflow						
Cash outflow (see monthly budget):	1,000	1,000	1,000			
Net cash on hand, end of month:	−1,000	−2,000	−3,000			

April

There's a saying that "April is the cruelest month." After four months in business and no dollar bill to frame and hang on the wall, you won't find much reason to argue with it. You make *four* sales—way above your monthly goal. However, you're still waiting for that first payment.

Month of: April
Sales Made: Four
Dollars Collected: Zero

	Jan	Feb	Mar	Apr	May	Jun
Inflow						
Cash on hand beginning of month:	0	–1,000	–2,000	–3,000		
Inflow:	—	—	—	—		
Outflow						
Cash outflow (see monthly budget):	1,000	1,000	1,000	1,000		
Net cash on hand, end of month:	–1,000	–2,000	–3,000	–4,000		

May

May. At last you get the check that pays you for the job you did back in February. Unfortunately, it's only $500. You still haven't broken even, though you're consistently closing three or more sales per month—well ahead of the sales goals you set back in January.

Assuming the worst—which I've done steadily in this section to add a healthy sense of realism—this is the lowest point on the chart for you. Negative $4,500 is what your initial capitalization must cover in order for you to remain in business over the first few months while you wait for revenue *you have coming* to materialize.

Month of: May
Sales Made: Three
Dollars Collected: 500

	Jan	Feb	Mar	Apr	May	Jun
Inflow						
Cash on hand beginning of month:	0	–1,000	–2,000	–3,000	–4,000	
Inflow:	—	—	—	—	500	
Outflow						
Cash outflow (see monthly budget):	1,000	1,000	1,000	1,000	1,000	
Net cash on hand, end of month:	–1,000	–2,000	–3,000	–4,000	–4,500	

The picture has become quite clear.

That last figure—$4,500—represents what *you must have in the bank* before you can even think about opening your doors on the first of January.

Of course, it's entirely possible that you may end up collecting that crucial 25 percent on agreement for every account. You may be able to implement terms that will make your financial position more attractive than the one I've outlined.

Then again, you may not.

June

The whole point of capitalizing your business is to ensure that you have enough—not almost enough—money. In other words, enough to make it to the point at which you take in sufficient revenue to keep your cash position from heading south all year long. In the sample months I've offered here, that point is June. And, as you'll see from the June scoreboard, reflecting the revenue from your sales in March, June is not when you start *making* money, it's the month you finally *turn the corner.*

Month of: June
Sales Made: Three
Dollars Collected: 1,500

	Jan	Feb	Mar	Apr	May	Jun
Inflow						
Cash on hand beginning of month:	0	–1,000	–2,000	–3,000	–4,000	–4,500
Inflow:	—	—	—	—	500	1,500
Outflow						
Cash outflow (see monthly budget):	1,000	1,000	1,000	1,000	1,000	1,000
Net cash on hand, end of month:	–1,000	–2,000	–3,000	–4,000	–4,500	–4,000

By now, you get the idea. The first few months represent the most potent threats to your business, and the goal of your capitalization plans should be to cover what you forecast to be *the lowest cash point you'll face*. Please note that you can be making sales like *crazy*—but not see the dollars for months. Too many months of waiting, too little capitalization, and you'll be out of business.

Following are the charts reflecting what the whole year might look like. (Of course, your actual year will look a *lot* better once your business has been properly capitalized!)

	First Six Months					
	Jan	Feb	Mar	Apr	May	Jun
Inflow						
Cash on hand beginning of month:	0	–1,000	–2,000	–3,000	–4,000	–4,500
Inflow:	—	—	—	—	500	1,500
Outflow						
Cash outflow (see monthly budget):	1,000	1,000	1,000	1,000	1,000	1,000
Net cash on hand, end of month:	–1,000	–2,000	–3,000	–4,000	–4,500	–4,000

	Last Six Months					
	Jul	Aug	Sep	Oct	Nov	Dec
Inflow						
Cash on hand beginning of month:	−4,000	−3,000	−2,500	−2,000	−1,500	0
Inflow:	2,000	1,500	1,500	1,500	2,500	1,500
Outflow						
Cash outflow (see monthly budget):	1,000	1,000	1,000	1,000	1,000	1,000
Net cash on hand, end of month:	−3,000	−2,500	−2,000	−1,500	0	500

Sales Goals and Business Plans

It should be clear, after that example, that your strategies and sales goals are far more than hypothetical objectives it would be nice to adhere to if you get the chance. They constitute honest, life-or-death business benchmarks that you have to take seriously. If you cannot or do not achieve your goals, you must do one of three things.

You can identify and solve a problem standing in the way; alter your approach to the business; or close up shop. Those are the options.

Think about it. That cash-flow scenario I just outlined was a pretty sobering item, don't you think? Well, here's the punch line: Once we got past February, *every month we discussed either met or exceeded the minimum number of sales necessary to defray monthly expenditures.*

What on earth will your first six months took like if you *don't* meet your sales goals? What if you underestimate the amount of time it takes you to complete a time-sensitive job, thereby winnowing away your precious marketing hours? What if you seriously underestimate your expenditures, and suddenly realize you must raise $2,000 a month instead of $1,000?

They'll be tough months. Far tougher than you'll want to endure, I guarantee you.

So take your projections, strategies, and goals *very* seriously. Know what you have to do every month to make things work. Know what you're spending. Know who else is offering the services you offer. Know what it is they offer that you don't, and vice versa. Above all else, *monitor your progress toward your goals,* and adjust accordingly if your plans don't seem to be working out.

CHAPTER 9

The End . . . or Your New Beginning?

Summing Up

And now comes the hard part—getting started.

Having read this book, you know that consulting is not for just anyone. Success in this field requires perseverance, determination, and a good measure of bravery, as well. Perhaps more importantly, consultants must be able to keep their efforts focused on the matters at hand—without getting sidetracked. When things aren't going quite according to plan (an eventuality you should certainly be prepared for), you must adjust your tactics and redouble your efforts, not only to solve the problems of your clients, but also to meet your own personal goals.

One of the beauties of this type of work, of course, is that you exercise a great deal of influence over your work environment. Many people who work in larger businesses encounter no small amount of frustration when they identify a problem at work, but have no opportunity to correct it. In consulting, the picture is quite different. If some part of the business is not proceeding along the lines you feel it should, you can change it—without having to check with the accounting or public relations department first. Whatever you come up with, the results will be yours to learn from, your experience to apply to the next problem.

Some people don't take to that kind of environment. The best consultants always do. For my own part, I wouldn't have it any other way.

One thing is certain. Once you enter this field, you'll get to know yourself quickly. From the first week of business onward, you'll be continuously defining and redefining who you are, what you do, and what you have to offer your clients. In the process, you'll probably call on strengths you never knew you had.

One final piece of advice: Be honest. In consulting, more so than many other businesses, *you* are the center of attention. Identify your positive points, but don't fool yourself into believing that your services will automatically be attractive to potential clients. What do you really have to offer? How do you implement your ideas? How is your service of genuine benefit to a client?

If you exaggerate what you can do, your client will, eventually, realize that he or she is not getting what was promised. That won't help your reputation. *Before you set up your practice* is the time to ask, "Do I really have a service that will help my clients? What is it? Can I deliver on my promises?"

A Guarantee

Whatever else can be said about consulting, I think I can guarantee one thing: You won't be bored. Though I've advised you to try to stick to a firm schedule, it's a solid bet you won't find yourself getting bogged down by routine. There'll be too much to do, more variety in your day than you know what to do with.

Though you'll work hard, the fact is consulting allows you a high degree of control over a very important factor—your own level of job satisfaction. There aren't many jobs that can promise that. That's why I love consulting, and why I'm confident you will too.

It's your business. Make the most of it!

CHAPTER 10

Forms to Build
a Business By

MAILING LIST

Page number   of
Date revised   /   /

Name	Address	Zip Code	Customer #	Date added	Mailing sent	Delete

DAILY APPOINTMENT LOG

Date   /   /

Client/Account	Service Type	Scheduled Time	Begin Time	End Time	Next Visit Date	Comments

Name: _____

Location: _____

CLIENT/PROSPECT CONTACT SUMMARY

Company: _____   **Representative:** _____

Contact: _____   **Product:** _____

Phone: /   -

Address: _____

_____

Date	Comment	When to call next?	Sale?

MONTHLY EXPENSE REPORT

For month of _____

Name _____

Date	Auto Mileage	Parking Tolls	Other Transportation	Meals	Lodging	Other (describe)	Other ($ amount)	TOTAL
1								
2								
3								
4								
5								
6								
7								
8								
9								
10								
11								
12								
13								
14								
15								
16								
17								
18								
19								
20								
21								
22								
23								
24								
25								
26								
27								
28								
29								
30								
31								

Total Mileage [____] X [____] Amount per mile

Subtotal [____]

Mileage costs [____]

TOTAL [____]

PURCHASE ORDER

Date / /
Order # _____

| Our Purchase Order Number must appear on all invoices, cases, packing lists, and correspondence |

To:

Date Wanted: / /
Terms: _____
Ship via: _____

Quantity	Item/Description	Price	Amount

_____
Authorized Signature

TOTAL COST

PRO-FORMA CASH FLOW CHART

	JAN	FEB	MAR	APR	MAY	JUN	JUL	AUG	SEP	OCT	NOV	DEC
INFLOW												
Cash on hand beginning of month:												
From sales:												
From interest, etc.:												
Loan proceeds:												
Inflow plus cash on hand:												
OUTFLOW												
Cost of goods sold:												
Direct payroll:												
Indirect payroll:												
Taxes, other than income tax:												
Sales expenses:												
Shipping, postage:												
Advertising, promotion:												
Office expenses:												
Travel, entertainment:												
Phone:												
Other utilities:												
Auto/truck:												
Insurance:												
Professional fees:												
Rent:												
Interest on loans:												
Taxes:												
Loan pay-down:												
Other:												
Cash outflow subtotal:												
Net cash on hand, end of month:												

SALESPERSON'S DAILY RECORD

SALESPERSON _____   Date   /   /

Company Name	Address/Telephone	Contact	Sold?	Comments

PAGE TOTALS: Contacts Made [   ]   Total Sales [   ]

Appendix

Organizations

Business Wire (media release outlet)
1990 S. Bundy
Los Angeles, CA 90025
310-820-9473
www.businesswire.com

D.E.I. Management Group
888 7th Avenue, 9th Floor
New York, NY 10106
1-800-224-2140
www.dei-sales.com

Executive Sales Briefing (newsletter)
888 7th Avenue, 9th Floor
New York, NY 10017
1-877-334-NEXT STEP
www.salesbriefing.com

International Guild of Professional Consultants
5703 Red Bug Lake Road
Winter Springs, FL 32708
407-644-6538
www.igpc.org

Institute of Management Consultants
1200 19th Street NW, Suite #300
Washington, D.C. 20036-2422
202-857-5334
www.imcusa.org

Management Consulting Network International
c/o TCF Consulting Group
P.O. Box 109
Lookout Mountain, TN 37350
708-820-2698
www.mcni.com

Index